The United States
and East Asia

The United States and East Asia

Richard W. Van Alstyne

W · W · NORTON & COMPANY · INC · New York

Frontispiece
1 Porcelain plate, with the arms of the United States
in the centre, made in China for export
to the United States. Early nineteenth century.

Picture Research: Georgina Bruckner

Copyright © 1973 Thames and Hudson Ltd, London
First American edition 1973
Printed in Switzerland by Roto-Sadag S.A., Geneva

ISBN 0 393 05491 8 (Cloth edition)
ISBN 0 393 09368 9 (Paper edition)

Contents

Preface

Since the Second World War a considerable body of monographic literature bearing on China and Japan in relation to the West has accumulated. Many of these books and articles are invaluable in that they succeed in placing these relationships in fresh historical perspective and in forcing Western students to revise their ideas about China and Japan, each with its own vast history and culture. For whatever new insights the present book provides much is due to the works of these other scholars. I also benefited from the manuscript collections in the Baker Library of Harvard University, and my thanks go to its staff for their gracious assistance. My long-time friend, Professor Barraclough, induced me to venture on this book, and he has followed it through chapter by chapter. The same word of appreciation is due to Mr Stanley Baron, managing editor of Thames and Hudson, who has been prompt and helpful in every respect.

For the past five years I have enjoyed a special relationship with Callison College, one of the cluster colleges of the University of the Pacific. Callison's uniqueness lies in its devotion to Asian studies, and so it seems fitting here to express my gratitude for the liberal provisions it has made in my behalf. And now that I am entering the twilight period of life it behoves me to put particular stress on the devotion of my dear wife, whose love is of the quality described in I Corinthians 13.

R. V. A.

20 July 1972

Through the centuries China, even more than India, has been a lure to foreign invaders. Historically it is a 'land of desire', as Hegel said of India. When, during the last quarter of the thirteenth century, the famed Venetian brothers Niccolo and Maffeo Polo, and Niccolo's son Marco, arrived for a lengthy sojourn, the Great Khan Kublai was completing the conquest begun by his grandsire, the Mongol chieftain Chinggis. Leading his horsemen from the steppes of Mongolia, Chinggis broke through the narrow pass of Nan-k'ou and in 1215, the year of Magna Carta in England, captured and burned Peking. The grandson, bent on restoring the empire under the new dynasty, rebuilt the city from the ground upwards.

Neither the first nor the last of the barbarians who invaded China from the north and the west, the Mongols (or Tartars, as Marco Polo calls them) ruled over a vast Eurasian empire of which China was only a part. Westward it reached deep into the heart of European Russia. The name China comes from an ancient people, the Ch'in, who were themselves among the early conquerors of the eastern lowlands. From their homeland in the valley of the Wei the Ch'in spread east and south down the Han river, a natural route for invasion which Kublai Khan followed a thousand years later and which the Chinese Communists were to follow again, after another seven hundred years, in their final push against the demoralized Nationalist army of Chiang Kai-shek. Marco Polo preferred the romantic sounding word Cathay as his name for China, and this name has been kept alive in the literature of the West. Marco Polo got the word from the Chitan, a nomadic Tartar tribe who preceded Chinggis Khan's hordes into China, only to be conquered themselves. A 'horde' was originally a mounted military unit which, under Mongol leadership, demonstrated its superiority everywhere in Asia and in Europe. It was the *Blitzkrieg* of the Middle Ages, conducted on many fronts. Marco Polo has a description of the horde's tactics:

When these Tartars come to engage in battle, they never mix with the enemy, but keep hovering about him, discharging their arrows first from one side and then from the other, occasionally pretending to fly, and during their flight shooting arrows backwards at their pursuers, killing men and horses, as if they were combating face to face. In this sort of warfare the adversary imagines he has gained a victory, when in fact he has

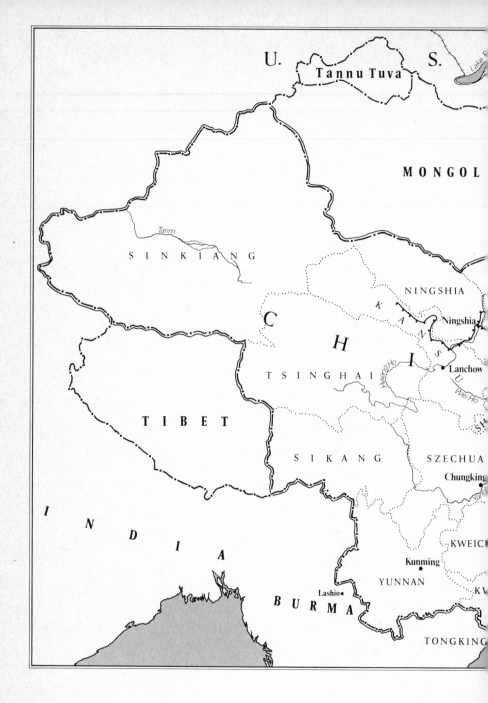

2 China and Japan, 1932.

lost the battle; for the Tartars, observing the mischief they have done him, wheel about, and renewing the fight, overpower his remaining troops, and make them prisoners in spite of their utmost exertions. Their horses are so well broken-in to quick changes of movement that, upon the signal given, they instantly turn in every direction; and by these rapid manœuvres many victories have been obtained.

On the plains of Manchuria in 1947 the Chinese Communists were to show the same tactical skill in deceiving and defeating their Nationalist rivals.

Traditionally an agricultural people to whom aggressive warfare was unnecessary and therefore repugnant, the Chinese nevertheless were not always the victims of these warlike barbarians. The emperor Wu-ti in the second century BC not only extended the 'Pax Sinica' so that it embraced all the country inside the Great Wall, which his predecessors had completed, but, copying Mongol tactics, penetrated deep into Outer Mongolia; and though he was forced into retreat, he was able to incorporate the strategic Ordos steppe (where the hordes, or *ordos*, congregated before launching an offensive into the Han valley) and enclose it inside the Wall. Since there were only five passes, including Nan-k'ou, where an enemy on horseback could get through – and then only when the Chinese garrison stationed at the pass defected – the Great Wall served China well. For fourteen hundred miles it ran through rugged country from Shan-hai-kuan at the edge of the sea to beyond the sources of the Wei in the far north-west. For the nomads of the steppes warfare was a way of life: they were herdsmen and shepherds whose foraging was mortgaged to the weather, and the farmlands of China were most vulnerable to their attacks when drought descended upon the plains. Even so, a 'friendly' Chinese frontier guard was necessary if numbers of barbarians were to get through. Trading along the frontier was normal, and small bands of barbarians were admitted to travel inside China; but large-scale raids and major invasions such as that staged by Chinggis Khan called for fifth column operations among the Chinese themselves. In other words, internal strife – a civil war, a rebellion, a mutiny among the soldiers, a betrayal in the Chinese field command – was a prerequisite of foreign conquest.

Whether under alien or under native rule, China was accustomed to despotic government. The family structure of society, devoted to its ancestors and obedient to the head of the household, tolerated none other; and the Chinese, the 'Men of Han' as they were known in the days of the first emperor, comprised one large, united family.

3 A Mongol horseman. Chinese drawing, Ming dynasty.

They were the Middle or Central Kingdom, taking strangers or barbarians only on their own terms. Confucian teaching demanded loyalty to the emperor, the Son of Heaven beyond whom there was no higher authority; and the mandarinate, or scholar-gentry class, which monopolized the offices of government at all levels, preserved unchanged the ancient Chinese tradition. The Mongol emperors ruled through this class whose influence, permeating all levels of society, was decisive in the continuous process of 'sinifying' all the peoples who dwelt within the boundaries of the empire.

The Chinese 'heaven' of course bore no resemblance to the Judaeo-Christian idea, nor did the Chinese 'state', for lack of a better term, compare in any way with the dynastic or nation state system of the West. The Son of Heaven (*t'ien-tzu*) was lord of lords, but he did not rule by 'divine right'. Confucius (Kung Fu-tzu) was the master sage,

4 The Great Wall. Engraving by T. Allom, 1843.

a teacher of Shantung province living in the sixth century BC whose sensible advice on human relations was so congenial to the Chinese mentality that to be a Chinese was the equivalent of being a Confucian. Such at least was invariably the case with the literate classes who ruled the country for two thousand years.

Reduced to its utmost simplicity, Confucianism was 'a civic order in communion, or rather in collaboration, with the cosmic order'. The Son of Heaven was the omnicompetent symbol of all power on earth, although to be sure the emperors differed greatly in ability through the centuries. Dynasties came and went, each new one starting off with a series of strong rulers only to enter a cycle of decay and corruption leading to rebellion and civil war. Indeed, some authorities have noted a correlation between population pressures and corruption in government: there were periods of prosperity accompanied by marked increases of population; but the productivity of the land remained constant, or rather it was subject to extreme fluctuations brought on by drought and frequent floods. Hard times, which meant famine, involved civic discontent which, when severe enough, could lead to the overthrow of the dynasty.

The Confucian ideal of government is to be found in Book II of the *Analects*. 'He who rules by moral force is like the pole star, which remains in its place while all the lesser stars do homage to it. . . . Govern the people by regulations, keep order among them by chastisements, and they will flee from you. . . . Govern them by moral force, keep order among them by ritual, and they will keep their self-respect and come to you of their own accord.' Socrates, between whom and Confucius there lay about a century in point of time, is the nearest Western prototype of the Chinese philosopher; but the Chinese, unlike the Greeks, had no system of pagan gods. Religious mysticism and idol worship were supplied through Buddhism, which crept into China from India through the oases of the Tarim basin. The ancient Silk Road traversed this basin, a formidable trade route linking China with Rome.

All three of the dynasties which we encounter in this book – the Mongol, the Ming and finally the Ch'ing – experienced the characteristic cycle of a rapid rise to power followed by a slow decline to the point of disintegration. Subsequent to its great success under Kublai Khan the Mongol empire began falling apart during the fourteenth century until, in 1368, it met extinction at the hands of a rebel chief, Chu Yüan-chang, from south of the Yangtze. Chu's family belonged to the impoverished native Chinese who suffered from the chronic epidemics and famines, but in his Bonaparte-like rise to power he hearkened to the Confucian rule of winning over his enemies. So China under the new dynasty, which adopted the name of Ming, was again ruled by Chinese, to remain so for 276 years. As a South Chinese, Chu moved the capital to Nanking on the Yangtze, or Long River; but his son moved back to Peking, the 'Violet-purple Forbidden City' made famous by the khans. Peking was within thirty miles of the Great Wall and protected from the barbarians by only two guarded passes, Nan-k'ou on the northwest and Shan-hai-kuan to the northeast. But the son, Yung-lo, reigned in the grand manner of empire, enriching the city with costly temples and a lavish new palace, carrying the war into distant Outer Mongolia, and in the south re-establishing suzerainty over the kingdoms of Indo-China.

Nanking and Peking stand for two different concepts of empire. Located on the south bank of the Long River, which dominates the heart of the country from the sea to the high mountains of the interior, Nanking symbolizes a self-centred empire content to live within its own borders. But in going boldly to Peking, the second of the Ming emperors adopted the ideas of the Great Khan, stressing the mission of China to bring civilization to the barbarians. Situated so close to a dangerous frontier, Peking signifies self-confidence and aggressiveness, for to the Chinese mind China and civilization are one and the same thing. Its vulnerable location makes Peking historically unique among the world's imperial capitals.

Considering the configurations of the Chinese sea coast, its numerous bays, river mouths and harbours so favourable to a maritime empire, one may well contrast the traditional Chinese indifference to seafaring enterprise with the maritime activities of other societies no better favoured by nature. Under Yung-lo, whose reign was contemporary with the earlier years of Prince Henry the Navigator of Portugal, China did embark temporarily on a programme of overseas expansion. For about twenty years, between 1405 and 1424, Chinese armadas sailed aggressively into the Indian Ocean, aiming at reducing Bengal and southern India and reaching as far as the Persian Gulf and the Red Sea. But material benefits from these expeditions were lacking: trade contacts were not established, the Chinese wanting no products that the lands of the Indian Ocean had to offer. No merchant class was created, no Chinese emigrants were dispatched overseas to found new colonies. So, except for the inshore coasting trade which, from the fifteenth century on, attracted numerous pirates among whom the Japanese pushed to the fore, the Chinese developed no capacity for seafaring. Had they done so, it is conceivable that they would have clashed head-on with the European adventurers advancing eastwards in the fifteenth and sixteenth centuries.

Chinese revolts took the form of banditry. In the rugged provinces of Shensi and Shansi to the west the bandit leaders could defy the imperial government and raid the lowlands for food. The Ming rulers having sunk to an all-time low in depravity and impotence, the garrison at Shan-hai-kuan opened the pass to the Manchu hordes who themselves had repudiated the suzerainty claimed by the Ming. At Shan-hai-kuan the Great Wall terminated in a fortress close to the water's edge, and whoever held this fortress possessed the key to invasion in either direction. In alliance with the garrison commander who opened the fortress, the Manchus overran northern China and established a new dynasty, which they called the Ch'ing. Aliens like the Mongols, though partially sinified under the Ming, the Manchus entered on the familiar cycle of Chinese régimes which carried them from strength through weakness and decay into the opening years of the twentieth century. Meanwhile Europeans, led by the Portuguese, 'discovered' China; and when, near the close of the eighteenth century, the Americans joined in the growing competition for the trade of South China, the Manchu régime was well past its peak and into the period of decay.

In the meantime, however, the dynasty had produced six strong rulers in succession, an unusual achievement among Chinese dynasties, and under them China expanded to an extent greater than at any time since the days of Kublai Khan. In 1750, one hundred years after

5 Kotowing official. Terracotta figure of the late T'ang dynasty.

its advent to power, the dynasty held suzerainty over all of Manchuria and Korea, Mongolia, Tibet, Vietnam, and even Nepal on the farther side of the Himalayas. Furthermore, it claimed tribute from the tribes occupying a broad fringe of territory south of Lake Baikal and east of the Caspian Sea. The tribute was an essential part of the traditional ritual by which non-Chinese peoples acknowledged membership of the civilized society of China; and in return they were recognized as no longer barbarians and were presented with gifts exceeding in value those which their messengers brought to the court of the Son of Heaven. The messengers – they were not ambassadors in the Western sense – performed the kotow, a ritual expressing homage and respect, a form of salutation which was 'merely a part of the universal order of Confucian ceremony which symbolized all the relationships of life. The emperor performed the kotow to Heaven and to his parents, the highest officials of the empire performed it to the emperor, and friends or dignitaries might even perform it mutually to each other. From a tribute envoy it was, therefore, no more than good manners'.[1]

Respect due from an inferior to his superior – from a child to his parent, from a servant to his master – was of the essence of Confucian philosophy. The kotow was the act of kneeling and touching the head to the ground, similar in meaning to the European code of chivalry and to the ritual expected of every Roman Catholic who, upon entering or leaving a church, bows or bends his knee to the altar. But Western envoys – ambassadors in their own eyes and in those of the governments which sent them – were blind to such parallels and refused to perform the kotow because to them it signified abject submission. A pompous American envoy in 1859 announced that he would kotow only to God and women, but his attitude was no different from the stiff refusals of British ambassadors who had gone before him. The Western state system, stressing independent sovereignty and equality among all states, had a ritual of its own and ran head-on against the Chinese system. Ideological differences between the two allowed no room for mutual understanding, and the Western distaste for the kotow was proof enough for the Chinese that Westerners really were barbarians.

All the many barbarians, from the Mongols and their several predecessors in ancient times to the Western Europeans of the sixteenth century, the Russians of the seventeenth century, and finally the Americans of the late eighteenth century, came to China. The Chinese did not go to them. China was the attraction, whether for purposes of outright conquest and settlement, of trade, of religious proselytizing, or of sheer curiosity. But the Chinese on their part felt no answering impulses. They did not go abroad to conquer, to establish trade outlets, to spread the teachings of Confucius. Even the aggressive moves of the early Ming emperors against their neighbours fit into this context. These were reprisals executed as a means of restoring and strengthening the tribute system. Tribute was the admission by the neighbour of his ethnic and cultural inferiority to China. This distinction between superiority and inferiority is the central myth of Chinese history. To the Chinese mind civilization and China were twin concepts. 'There was only civilization and barbarism, and they were conceptually related in that they defined each other – that is, what was not civilized was barbaric!' Or, to express it differently, civilization was 'an empire without neighbours'.[2] To be sure, this unique ethnocentrism was inseparable from military power and political influence. The sedentary populations of Korea and South-East Asia were held tightly to the imperial authority, the nomads of the north and west less so.

Europeans, with whom the Americans were identified, were the 'red-haired barbarians', physically distinguishable from the customary types of inferiors: 'Their flesh is dazzling white, and their noses are lofty . . . their custom is to esteem women and think lightly of men. . . . The men are violent and tyrannical and skilled in the use of weapons. They wear short coats and tip their black felt hats as a sign of politeness.'

The advent of these strangers, whose presence became more menacing in the eighteenth century, created fresh embarrassments for the Chinese. For the first time China was threatened from the sea; all the ancient relationships were land-based, but the Chinese had no experience and no means of warding off these new invaders. The fiction of ethnic superiority remained fixed, but the power to make it good was lacking. Whence these new barbarians came was something of a mystery. They were known to live along the shores of the Great Western Ocean, somewhere beyond the 'Little Western [that is, Indian] Ocean'. North America was thought of as a small, isolated island about ten days' sailing time to the west of England.

When Lord Macartney arrived at Tientsin in 1793, accompanied by a numerous staff and bearing gifts valued at £15,000 for the emperor, he was naturally received as a messenger from a new tributary state. The Chinese treated him with the customary politeness and gave him lessons in the performance of the kotow. He came as an ambassador of the Crown, although his mission was financed by the East India Company. He insisted that he did no more than bend his knee to the emperor, as he would to his own sovereign, but the Chinese preferred to believe that he had met the requirements of the ritual. The emperor sent a gracious reply to King George III, but the letter must have startled His Majesty's ministers when translated for them in distant Whitehall. 'I have already taken note of your respectful spirit of submission,' wrote the emperor. 'I do not forget the lonely remoteness of your island, cut off from the world by intervening wastes of sea.'[3] Perhaps the irony in this message was unconscious. Macartney wanted diplomatic representation European-style, a printed tariff, open ports at Ningpo and Tientsin, and island depots near Canton and Chusan – substantially all that was extorted by force half a century later. But at the time Macartney (or rather his sponsor, the East India Company) got nothing for his pains.

17

6 Haida Indian carvings (*c.* 1840) of American visitors to the Charlotte Islands. They give an indication of the attire of the American sailors and merchants who arrived in China during the second quarter of the nineteenth century.

2 The Americans arrive in China

'China is the first for greatness, riches, and grandeur, of any country ever known.'[1] The statement might have come from Marco Polo in 1272 when he first viewed the great city and palace of Peking. Actually it was the opinion of Amasa Delano of New York City, expressed more than five hundred years later after visiting Canton. Delano was an American shipmaster, among the early birds of the 1790s who capitalized on the need of the Chinese for furs and sealskins. Delano was a great-grandfather of Franklin Delano Roosevelt, and he and his son Warren founded the family fortune in dealing with the Hong merchants of Canton. President Roosevelt, as we shall see, liked to boast of the adventures of these ancestors of his

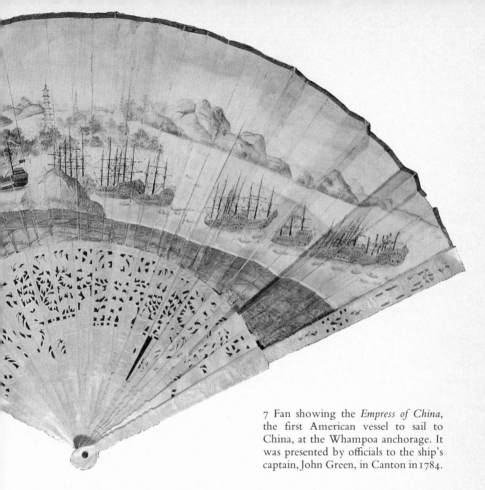

7 Fan showing the *Empress of China*, the first American vessel to sail to China, at the Whampoa anchorage. It was presented by officials to the ship's captain, John Green, in Canton in 1784.

and to give them credit for his wartime notion of China in firm partnership with the United States. As China merchants, the careers of the two Delanos spread over a period of half a century. Warren Delano became a partner in the house of Russell, foremost among the American firms trading to China after 1830. The firm's net profit for 1842, the last year of the Opium War, amounted to $130,000, a figure so pleasing that Warren, who was now thinking of retiring, hoped that it could be made the annual take 'for the next five hundred years'.[2]

The sale of sea otter pelts and sealskins to the Chinese constituted a most important trade secret which enabled the Americans to push up to second place in the foreign commerce of China. Only the British, among the Western merchants, were ahead of them. Furs gave the

19

Americans considerable relief from the burden of specie payments if they were to buy direct from the Chinese the many things that the West desired from the East in ever-increasing amounts. Silken goods, nankeens, and especially teas – Bohea, Hyson, Soochong – topped the list. In the eighteenth century tea rose to first place in popular demand, in America as well as in Britain. In the forty years between 1761 and 1800, the English East India Company's tea shipments from Canton increased from 2,626,000 lb to 23,300,000 lb. James Boswell in his *London Journal* for 1762-63 makes it evident that he never passed a day without enjoying 'a cup of tea'; and in America the tea merchants managed to take advantage of the competition between the English and Dutch East India Companies, smuggling in Dutch tea at a price below the English. British government efforts in 1773 to thwart the smugglers led to the notorious 'Boston Tea Party'. But there was a long list of other goods for which only China could satisfy Western tastes – precious hand-made and hand-painted china-ware and other porcelain, jade, chessmen, toys, artificial flowers and other objects for the homes of the well-to-do. In rejecting Lord Macartney's request for more liberal trade relations, the Emperor Chien Lung replied that China possessed all 'things in prolific abundance' and needed nothing from the outside world.

When in 1784 American merchant ships started coming to China independently of the British, they of course participated in the Canton system. Trade, like other relations with barbarians, was in the tradition of favours granted by the dynasty; and to cope with it, the Chinese maintained a customs bureau at Canton headed by a superintendent (*Hoppo*) and authorized thirteen Hong merchants to deal with the foreigners. There were thirteen factories or compounds ('ghettoes' in current American terminology) built along the water-front known as the Whampoa anchorage outside the walled city of Canton; and in these factories lived the foreign merchants and their employees under conditions prescribed by the Chinese. Thus the Canton system was a variation upon the time-honoured tribute system; but in the course of the eighteenth century, trade with the Western world was having a growing effect upon the economy of China and contributing increasingly to the revenues of the official bureaucracy, from the emperor's court down to the Hong merchants. In other words, the lofty attitude assumed by the emperor in 1793 was anachronistic, a truth which the Chinese were slow to grasp.

The avid demand for furs, which the Americans were best fitted to supply, is a case in point. Pelts had long come across the frontier in the north from Russia, and were utilized by the northern Chinese in garment-making; and the potential of this trade became apparent when the mariners sailing with Captain James Cook on the last of his three great voyages earned a quick profit at Canton from the sale of sea otter pelts that they had obtained in Russian waters.

Cook's explorations in the Pacific had attracted international attention on their own account. While in Paris to negotiate peace with Britain in 1783, John Adams speculated on the possibilities for a new international rivalry developing in the North Pacific. 'What should hinder the Empress of Russia,' he remarked in his diary, 'from establishing a trading city on the Sea of Kamchatka and opening a commerce with Peking, Nankin, and Canton, the cities of China? It is so near the islands of Japan, the Philippines, the Moluccas, that a great scene may one day be opened here.' Thomas Jefferson on his part revealed the mercantile spirit: foreign trade was an instrument of national power, and Jefferson declared himself eager to get ahead of the British in the India and China trade. One way to do it was to pioneer a new trade route shortening the distance between the United States and China. Jefferson caught the idea for such a route from John Ledyard, a Yankee corporal of marines who had sailed under Cook. Ledyard undertook to blaze a trail across Siberia and then hopefully cross the Bering Sea and work his way home to the United States from some point on the west coast of North America. And from another American, who in 1786 returned from a very profitable voyage to China, Jefferson got the idea of the 'open door'. 'The commerce with the East,' remarked this merchant, who published a book on his experience, 'shou'd if it were possible be made common by all the powers of inconsiderable influence in that country.'[3]

For about thirty years, from 1790 to 1820, American mariners and merchants owed their great successes in the China trade to the herds of seals and sea otter they found everywhere from the Falkland Islands in the South Atlantic to remote islands in the southern Indian Ocean. The Hong merchants were always ready buyers, while keeping ahead of the foreigners in setting the prices they would pay. Sealskins ranged in price from forty-two cents to $1.12 on the Canton market. Captain Daniel Greene of Connecticut pioneered the hunt among the Falkland Islands in 1792, and enormous numbers of seals were found ready for the slaughter on the little known islands off the coasts of Chile and Peru. Amasa Delano was a frequent visitor to these waters. So was Captain Edmund Fanning who, during his sealing expeditions, took pains to chart islands and reefs over immense stretches of the Pacific Ocean. 'We passed thousands and thousands of seals, so tame, as almost to encircle the ship', reported another mariner while sailing through Bass Strait between Australia and Tasmania.[4] Nevertheless, competition was so feverish that new habitats were not always reported, and sometimes the same island was 'discovered' more than once by different shipmasters. Captain David Porter, commanding an American frigate on the look-out in the South Atlantic and the Pacific during the War of 1812 for British vessels he might capture, was diligent in spreading false information. At the end of the war Porter was inspired to write a report to the President on the commercial empire the United States was developing in the Pacific. Russia, Japan, China, not to mention the islands, were all neighbours of the United States, he told the President. Japan especially aroused his interest: it was a nation of 'rooted prejudices', but its trade was worth having; and to 'make that people known to the world' would be a great achievement.[5]

American vessels unloaded 2,500,000 sealskins at Canton between 1792 and 1812. How many millions of sea otter pelts reached the same destination seems not to be on record. The sea otter was in special demand for its beauty and its warmth, both ornamental and useful. It swam the waters of the Pacific Coast, all the way from Lower California to the Aleutian Islands; and the hunt for this creature familiarized American masters and crews with this thousand-mile stretch of inviting coast. The slaughter was devastating, so that after 1820 delays and uncertainties in locating the prey brought diminishing returns to the business. Sealing and sea otter hunting were dead well before the middle of the century.

Sandalwood proved equally enticing to Chinese buyers, but the exploitation of this beautiful grained wood was even more short-lived than the fur trade. Americans learned of it from the natives of Tonga, who extracted a scented oil from the wood, and the Chinese ground the heart of the wood into a fine powder for incense. Scarcity kept the price stable at $17.00 per picul ($133^{1}/_{3}$ lb) during the comparatively short life of the trade. Fiji was the original source, but within the eight years from 1805 to 1812 the supply was exhausted. The Marquesas Islands were sought out next, but the Sandwich Islands (i.e. Hawaii) proved even better. American merchants made money out of sandalwood for the next ten years, but by 1825 the business was practically dead. Hawaii had many other attractions, however. Its central location made it an entrepôt for the Pacific coast

8 Factories of foreign powers at Canton, *c.* 1800. Chinese painting on glass.

of North America on the one hand and for East Asia on the other. It was drawing merchants, seamen, permanent settlers and missionaries from the United States. By 1810 Honolulu was an established community, and the process of transforming a native Polynesian kingdom into an American colony was under way.

The German explorer Otto von Kotzebue, on a four-year voyage of discovery for the tsar, remarked on the burst of activity that followed the end of the great wars in Europe. Von Kotzebue perceived the connection between missionary activity, commerce and political ambition. 'The rage for converting savage nations is now spreading over the whole South Sea', he observed, 'and causes much mischief, because the missionaries do not take pains to make men of them before they make them Christians, and thus, what should bring them happiness and tranquillity becomes the source of bloody wars; as, for example, in the Friendly Islands, where the Christians and heathens reciprocally try to exterminate each other.' California and the Sandwich Islands complemented each other. California could develop into the granary and market of the northern coasts and the general resort of ships; the islands, on their part, would be best off as a free port and staple of all the navigators of the Pacific. 'But should any foreign power conceive the foolish idea of taking possession of them, the jealous vigilance of the Americans, who possess the almost exclusive commerce of these seas, and the secure protection of England, would not be wanting to frustrate the undertaking.'[6]

With the London Missionary Society (founded in 1795) setting the example, the New England churches established in 1810 the American Board of Commissioners for Foreign Missions and shortly thereafter made Hawaii their first outpost. Hawaii continued to be the object of their major effort – the Bible was translated into the native tongue, schools were set up for the native children, and, when in 1842 the moment arrived for formally reconstructing the native government as a constitutional monarchy, it was the New England missionaries, now permanent residents of the islands, who accomplished this feat. Naturally Hawaii was the hub for American missionary work on other islands of the Pacific and also among the Indians of the Oregon country on the mainland. In Boston the *Missionary Herald*, which began publication in 1805, followed the work of the English missionary Robert Morrison in China and declared that America must assume its share in evangelizing the world. The millennium would arrive in two hundred years, and by that time America would exceed Europe in population, in wealth and political influence, and in

9 The missionary Robert Morrison and his two Chinese assistants translating the Bible into Chinese. Engraving after a painting by George Chinnery.

purity of faith and moral deportment. As for China, where the population was known to be hostile to foreigners, it was 'an empire so vast, so populous, and so idolatrous that it cannot be mentioned by Christians without exciting sentiments of the deepest concern.'[7]

Another American writer, William Davis Robinson, a merchant who had taken part in the Mexican rebellion against Spain, described the geography of Mexico, noted that that country could never rival the United States, and remarked on how America, through geographical proximity to Asia, could force changes on that continent too. Maritime superiority would supply the means. Robinson was much interested in the possibilities of an inter-oceanic route and what it would do in linking the United States to Oregon on the one hand and to China on the other. And how could Spain expect to hold on to Cuba, Puerto Rico and the Philippines, stepping-stones for American power in the Pacific? A response to this query was to be deferred for some seventy-five years.

But more important at the time in shaping an imperial American ideology directed at the Pacific and China was the concept of 'the North American road to India', the combined transcontinental and trans-Pacific route which had been in Jefferson's mind since 1787. Considering the maritime activity in the Pacific and the extent to which the Sandwich Islands were sliding under American influence, an overland route to the Columbia river would open the way for diverting the trade of the Orient from Europe to the United States. The famed Lewis and Clark expedition, sent out by Jefferson, opened such a route in 1804-06. Untold wealth and power and a virtual stranglehold on the world's commerce lay within the American reach. Thomas Hart Benton, the eminent senator from Missouri, was now talking in this sense, the newspapers of St Louis were playing up their city as the future 'Venice of the New World', and the government of President John Quincy Adams was working to oust the British from the Pacific Northwest. Once the ocean frontage with its alluring harbours was under American control, the China trade would belong to the United States.

For many years thereafter this idea remained uppermost among American expectations. After leading a voyage of exploration around the world in 1838-42 and writing five thick volumes on the subject, published and circulated under government auspices, Commander Charles Wilkes felt confident that California and Oregon would combine to form a powerful maritime nation. Two of the finest ports in the world would be theirs: the straits of Juan de Fuca and

San Francisco Bay. These two regions, Wilkes concluded, had

everything to make them increase, and keep up an intercourse with the whole of Polynesia, as well as the countries of South America on the one side, and China, the Philippines, New Holland, and New Zealand, on the other. Among the latter before many years, may be included Japan. Such various climates will furnish the materials for a beneficial interchange of products, and an intercourse that must, in time, become immense; while this western coast, enjoying a climate in many respects superior to any other in the Pacific, possessed as it must be by the Anglo-Norman race, and having none to enter into rivalry with it . . . is evidently destined to fill a large place in the world's future history.[8]

We shall continue to meet this theme, with some variation of language, until well into the twentieth century.

Furs and skins were prime assets, as we have seen, in giving American merchants their start in the China trade, but even so there was always a deficit in the balance of payments for the teas and costly merchandise marketed throughout the whole of the Western world. The real profits of the China trade derived from the sale of Chinese goods in the West, and all the Western merchants scrambled for things they hoped would appeal to the Chinese taste. Taking advantage of the ice they could cut from the lakes and ponds of New England in winter, Boston men even ventured into an ice trade. By packing blocks of ice in straw and stowing it in the holds of fast sailing vessels, shippers managed, in spite of two crossings of the Equator, to save enough ice to sell to the Cantonese as a novelty product. As they began to face increasing costs in obtaining furs and skins after 1820, the American China merchants found themselves in the same dilemma as other Western traders in Canton. Silver in various forms could always be relied upon, whether in ingots or in miscellaneous coins such as Mexican dollars, Venetian ducatoons, French crowns, German and Scandinavian rix-dollars, or Indian rupees. Chinese prices were in taels – one tael equalled an ounce of silver – but foreign coins had to be tested for fineness and weight. Obviously there were limits to the West's capacity for exporting silver. The British hoped for a large market for woollens, but the Chinese demand was at best only moderate.

Opium was the one commodity that enjoyed an expanding market in China, although why it should have taken hold more in China than elsewhere remains unexplained. The Dutch first created a market for it in the seventeenth century, and then the Portuguese took the lead in selling it through their peninsular station at Macao. It was orig-

10 Chinese opium smokers. Engraving by T. Allom, 1843.

inally thought to be a protection against malaria; the fatal demand for it as a habit-forming drug mushroomed in the eighteenth century. Writing to his wife from Canton in 1843, the Boston merchant Paul S. Forbes gives a graphic account of a Chinese addict: 'He must smoke every day or he can't walk about! His nerves are so unstrung that the tears roll down his cheeks, but as soon as he has smoked his first quantum, his energy returns.'[9]

Paul Forbes was one of a large family of Boston merchants who were in business in Canton for some years before and some years after the Opium War of 1839-42. The family came originally from Aberdeenshire in northern Scotland. In Canton the Forbes brothers were at first associated with Bryant and Sturgis and then with Russell and Company, both of whom were leaders among the American China firms.

Americans trading in the eastern Mediterranean in the 1790s realized they could buy Turkish opium and sell it in China. 'I am very much in favour of investing heavily in opium,' declared Stephen Girard, the Philadelphia banker, in January 1805. It would fetch a good price in China. Turkish opium continued to enjoy favour, and all the leading American firms handled it; but Indian opium did much better, possibly because costs could be cut by the much shorter voyage from Calcutta or Bombay. Bengal, or Patna, opium was declared a monopoly of the East India Company in 1773, but Malwa opium from the native states of western India remained competitive until 1830. The Chinese authorities tried by simple prohibition to stop it, but the popular demand for the drug continued to spiral and spread from the sea ports into the interior. In 1834 Turkish opium sold in Canton at $620.00 per picul, Malwa opium realized $600.00 and Patna $530.00. Price fluctuations could be sudden, contingent upon amounts brought in. John Murray Forbes, who was handling the stuff for the American company Bryant and Sturgis at Canton, realized he could not compete with the product from India.

Opium was by then the leader among foreign imports into China: 35,000 chests, weighing 133 pounds (one picul) each, were getting past customs illegally, but by 1839 the figure rose to 40,000. Opium was the chief trouble-breeder, but it was also the greatest money-maker and it affected the economy of India, the producing country, as well as of China, the consuming country. It was the principal source of the East India Company's income, but the Company depended upon the peasant farmers who grew it. Fearful of forfeiting its privileges in China, the Company took care not to allow its own vessels to carry the stuff, but other shipowners took the risks and among these American dealers assumed the lead. In the 1830s the Scottish firm of Jardine, Mathieson and Company was the largest dealer in opium, with Russell and Company of Boston and Providence, Rhode Island, third. Swift disposal of the stuff to smugglers along the coast north of Canton was sufficient inducement to the latter to pay the higher freights charged by the fast clipper ships, especially built for the India trade.

In Canton the Hong merchants were too vulnerable to high fines and severe punishments to risk personal involvement. Thus Houqua, reputed to be the richest man in the world and the merchant with whom the American firms did business, refused to handle opium; but his attitude did not discourage Russell and Company from engaging in it. Chinese authorities upon occasion were capable of imposing 'exquisite punishments', meaning strangling, upon offenders. But crackdowns were too rare and too capriciously conducted to hamper the highly efficient racket which protected the traffic. Ocean-going vessels discharged their opium chests at Lintin before

11 A painting by George Chinnery of Houqua, the wealthy Hong merchant at Canton.

proceeding to their regular berth at the Whampoa higher up the Pearl river. At Lintin the bootlegging began, mostly at the hands of native Chinese who paid the importer in silver and, with the chests packed away on small boats, set forth to market the product in the smaller towns and villages along the coast. All the boats were heavily armed, their valuable cargoes attracting attack from the numerous Chinese pirate ships lying in wait among the islands. Foreigners and Chinese smugglers, pirates and government officials, were all mixed up together in this lucrative traffic.

In all other respects too the foreigners, while in stiff competition among themselves, were associated together in a common cause, which was directed at making the maximum profit out of the China trade. The British were well in the lead of the other 'barbarians', the Americans placed second and competing with the British for the carrying trade between China, India and Western Europe. In Canton the Americans commonly settled their accounts with the Hong merchants by drawing bills on London, and a profitable trade in bills developed. Houqua, the wealthy Hong merchant, had funds invested in America, the keeping of which he entrusted to the Forbes brothers; they also handled his tea shipments to London on commission. American vessels frequently carried cargo on round-the-world voyages, competing with British Indiamen in the delivery of tea to the British home market. The new clipper ships, built in New England yards, entered this trade with great success. Paul Forbes thrilled to the news received in Canton that one of these graceful vessels, the *Antelope*, had reached Bombay in thirty-two days, 'the shortest passage yet made – beating all other clippers both ways'.

The American share of the opium trade with India approached one-tenth. Bennett Forbes, elder brother to Paul, described for the latter's benefit the dangers of this trade as he saw it in April 1839. Alarmed at the ravages the drug was making on the population, the imperial Chinese authorities had been trying for three years to suppress it. But corruption of the bureaucracy at all levels was so great that honest officials were meeting with little success. Within twelve miles of Canton government boats were taking opium on board and selling it. The imperial commissioner, Lin Tse-hsü, now brought matters to a head in a demand that all opium in the hands of foreigners at Canton be surrendered; and Captain Charles Elliott, the British representative, complied. Lin seized and destroyed 20,286 chests, of which, according to Forbes, about 1500 were American-owned.

The Opium War, which broke out as a result of this crisis, was a British war with China, but it is not possible to separate the Americans from it or from its consequences. Only the British government had a policy toward China which, as we have seen, dated from the embassy of 1793. British efforts to convince the Chinese of the superiority of the European state system, with its corollary of diplomatic relations among equals, having been rebuffed, the Chinese system of dealing only with inferiors had continued to prevail. At Canton the *Hoppo* (the superintendent of the customs) and his staff collected duties not from the foreigners direct, but through the Hong merchants from whom he extorted 'squeeze'. It was normal for the foreigners to deal only with the Hong, and if any of them desired direct communication with the *Hoppo*, he had to do it on the basis of a humble petition accompanied by a ritual that would demonstrate his inferiority.

The East India Company managed its business affairs with the Hong through a select committee residing at its factory at the Whampoa anchorage, and its dominant position was such that other traders, including the Americans, were able to secure for themselves whatever terms were granted the Honourable Company. In other words what was known in the West as 'most-favoured-nation treatment' functioned at Canton on a *de facto* basis. The practice of equal treatment of all barbarian tribute-bearers was fundamental to Chinese tradition.

When in 1834, however, Parliament abolished the Honourable Company's monopoly, this working arrangement no longer obtained: under the new competitive system each of the 'foreign devils' had to negotiate separately through his Hong merchant. The American firm, Russell and Company, appears to have fared well through ties of personal friendship with Houqua, 'a right good old fellow' of seventy-four. Houqua had been a Hong merchant for half a century, 'an intelligent, high-minded liberal Chinaman', Paul Forbes wrote to his wife, who 'would honour any country'. Jardine-Mathieson and Dent and Company were the two British firms superseding the East India Company in the China trade. In place of the Company the Chinese in 1834 had asked the British government to send a 'head man', a type of person experienced in dealing with Arab traders. Being merely an agent, a 'head man' would not violate Chinese tradition. But Lord Palmerston, the Foreign Secretary, dispatched a fully accredited envoy whose expectations of being received by the *Hoppo* and the government of Kwangtung province in the name of the emperor remained unfulfilled. Failing to obtain permission to enter the city of Canton, Lord Napier, Palmerston's envoy, retired in disgrace to Macao and died soon after.

The outbreak of hostilities over the opium crisis in 1839 led to the seizure by British forces of five Chinese ports designated by William Jardine as advantageous to future trade: Swatow, Amoy (known for its spacious harbour and as an established centre for the opium trade), Foochow, Ningpo and Shanghai. A British threat to occupy Nanking induced the imperial authorities to send a skilful diplomat named Ch'i-ying to negotiate. Ch'i-ying yielded the five ports and, in addition, ceded the island of Hongkong as a free port and agreed to the payment of an indemnity. Ch'i-ying managed to stretch out the negotiations for a year, and in spite of the British demonstration of superior force he preserved the Chinese tradition of making concessions to the barbarian in return for tribute. Ceremony and the exchange of elaborate gifts marked the course of the negotiations. The 'sea barbarians' differed from earlier land barbarians in that they wanted trade, not territory; and China, during its chronic periods of weakness, was accustomed to making concessions.

Paul Forbes, arriving at Macao in May 1843 at the end of a 111-day voyage from Boston which he thought to be excellent time, witnessed an outbreak of xenophobic feeling among the people of Canton which made it apparent that foreigners would still be confined to their factories. Forbes comprehended the difficulty of reconciling Chinese with Western attitudes, registered indignation at the arrogance the British had displayed, and doubted Western claims of superiority. Noting that white was the emblem of mourning in China, in contrast to black as the colour of the West, he remarked, 'So do customs differ and opinions too. Now China is the most ancient country known and from which we have taken half of our customs, and who shall decide whether they are not as right as we are. In the sciences and arts they are far behind us, but in morals our equals, and have been till within a century practically our superiors for 2000 years!'

Forbes's broad-mindedness, however, did not affect his nose for business. He was both a member of Russell and Company and United States consul at the same time. Among the trading nations this practice was common for some years. When Shanghai was opened, Russell and Company had the consulate there too. Occasionally Forbes was conscious of his consular role, as when he was obliged to take note of the superstitions of the local populace. An arrow, used by him as a weather vane at the top of the flagpole, aroused fears in the crowd that it would bring death to anyone who happened to be in the direction in which it pointed. The mob grew restless, but only after three of the Hong merchants had protested to Forbes would he consent to remove the arrow. 'But what will our missionaries say,' he complained, 'when they hear the Consul has respected this superstition of the Heathen! This all appears ridiculous enough here and will be more so at home, but when you see the most respectable men believing and crowds of Chinamen gazing at the staff with a kind of dread, the case is altered somewhat.' Forbes was in trouble with the *Hoppo* too through refusing to accept the latter's characterization of foreigners as 'barbarians'.

After the war Russell and Company had reopened their opium business, and by 1843 it was large enough to justify the assignment of a special vessel to trade with the firm's correspondents in India. At the Whampoa its general business was so good that seven of the company's ships sailed fully laden in the single month of December. By this time Sir Henry Pottinger, the British diplomat, had reached a final peace settlement with Ch'i-ying. Hongkong was now a free port without any customs duties, a storage centre for opium on its way to the coastal trade, and a haven for Christian missions; and the five Chinese treaty ports were opened to unrestricted international trade subject only to a low uniform tariff of five per cent *ad valorem*, which the British calculated to be high enough to meet the costs of a native Chinese collectorate. The French and American governments sent diplomatic missions of their own. The French, having very little trade at stake, concentrated on freedom of religion: missionaries were allowed to go into the interior, wearing Chinese garb, and all Chinese were permitted to worship according to Christian rites.

Of the American emissary Caleb Cushing, who came from Forbes's home state, Forbes at first expected great things. He soon changed his mind, however: Ch'i-ying managed Cushing adroitly, giving him nothing that was not already written into the British treaty and dashing his hopes of paying an official visit to Peking. Cushing, a lawyer, could point with pride to his legal skill in drafting a clause relating to extraterritoriality, and on paper he outlawed the opium traffic. But these provisions did not influence Russell and Company, who continued to compete for the opium business; and since the company controlled the consulates at Canton and Shanghai, it had no interest in the suppression of smuggling. Moreover, foreigners venturing beyond the limits of the factories did so at their peril. 'I have had an anxious time of it,' Forbes reported to his brother in July 1844, 'and for a week we did our counting with a musket alongside each desk and a pair of pistols in our pockets.'

'Anti-foreignism' – the peculiar brand of Chinese xenophobia which Forbes and his associates had good reason to fear – is still an untilled field for Western scholarship. Recurrent outbreaks of it against the 'foreign devils' had occurred since the first coming of the Portuguese; in Forbes's day it took the form of attacks on foreigners who ventured beyond the limits of the compounds. Missionaries felt the danger as keenly as the merchants; and when foreigners took advantage of the new treaty ports, notably Amoy, they took their lives in their hands. An American mission opened at this port commented on the dangers of mob violence. To the evils of opium-running was added, in the 1850s, a flourishing trade in coolies, of which Amoy was the centre. The business of securing batches of coolies, by kidnapping or otherwise, arose from the demand for cheap labour that came from the gold mines of California and Australia, from the guano deposits of Peru, and from the sugar plantations of the West Indies. Russell and Company competed for this business, contracting to carry shiploads of coolies across the Pacific at $30.00 per head.

This xenophobia was the forerunner of Chinese nationalism at the popular level. In the meantime the ruling mandarins continued to nurse their illusions of the superiority of the Middle Kingdom and of its capacity to tame the barbarian. Actually the efforts to 'tame' were attempts to appease. The new barbarians, led by the British, nourished ideas of their own superiority and could not dream of submitting to cultural assimilation by China. This basic fact the Chinese mind could not accept, but neither could it hope to tame the new barbarians as it had the invaders of the past. The barbarians from the West had the power and the disposition to impose upon the Chinese as much as they liked.

To the British and the Americans free trade and the Christian religion were the hallmarks of civilization. Rutherford Alcock, the forceful British consul at Shanghai, and his American colleague, Edward Cunningham, were agreed on this. China was doomed to succumb to the superior power of the West; philanthropy and commercial advantage were virtuous ends; and it was the mission of Britain and America to guide and enlighten the Chinese. The three leading American Protestant missionaries, Samuel Wells Williams, Elijah Bridgman and Dr Peter Parker, who entered China in the early 1830s, were certain of this too. All three came from New England and were career missionaries, remaining in China for most of their lives. Williams wrote a masterly two-volume work, *The Middle Kingdom*, first published in 1848 and again in 1883. When he arrived he was a 'foreign devil', but forty years later he was received by the Son of Heaven on a footing of perfect equality. He would have been less than human if he had not regarded this change as a triumph. The Chinese were irreligious, he conceded, but nevertheless they were getting the message. Christian missions, railways, telegraphs and manufactures were the instruments of civilization. Bridgman followed in the footsteps of his English predecessor, Robert Morrison, in translating the Bible into Chinese. Parker, a medical missionary, operated a hospital in Canton and developed positive ideas on American official policy toward China. As United States commissioner (the American substitute for minister), he forcibly argued that the United States should take Formosa as an equivalent

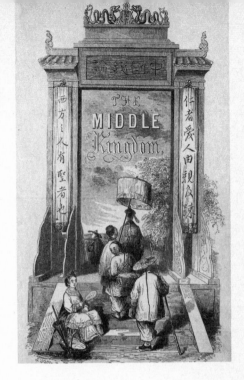

12 Title-page of *The Middle Kingdom* (1848), by the missionary S. Wells Williams.

to Hongkong and ally with Britain and France in resorting to war against China in 1856. All of the missionaries were aware of the ravages of opium, and, while they deplored it, it did not shake their confidence in the moral superiority of the West; nor did xenophobia, to which they themselves were subject, dampen their enthusiasm for converting 'the heathen'.

John Quincy Adams, the American elder statesman, and John Bowring, the British diplomat contemporary with Peter Parker in China, furnish interesting illustrations of this coincidence of Anglo-American attitudes. Commerce, the Protestant faith, and relentless political pressure on the Chinese were the sure means of extending the blessings of civilization. Adams was a doughty advocate of the Western principle of sovereignty and independence, and with unvarnished language he took up the British cause in the Opium War. China's attitude was anti-social, unrighteous because it violated the Christian precept to 'love thy neighbour', anti-commercial and accordingly immoral – 'an enormous outrage upon the rights of human nature, and upon the first principles of the rights of nations'.[10] Bowring, the hymn writer, held to a lifelong conviction of the virtue of free trade, and as British envoy to China it was thus natural for

35

him to push for more treaty ports and the right of Great Britain to full diplomatic recognition. He was a career man with a background of practical experience in China, and he studied that country with much the same intentness as did S. Wells Williams. Holding a free hand in China in 1854 and having the co-operation of the American commissioner, Robert McLane, Bowring put through an important change in the Chinese customs and pursued policies that led to the Second China War.

Both merchants and missionaries took swift advantage of the opportunities available to them at Hongkong and the new treaty ports. Hongkong's population rocketed to 25,000 by the summer of 1843, the city outstripping Macao and Canton as an entrepôt for Kwangtung province and attracting to its harbour vessels of all descriptions, including Chinese junks, engaged in the coastal trade. American missionaries in China now numbered fifty-nine, and were sending appeals to headquarters in Boston that many more should answer the call. Canton was still tightly closed in 1849, but the missionaries were sure the hostility, most virulent at that port, would die down: the Chinese would learn to reconcile themselves to a situation they could not alter. Of the new treaty ports Amoy and Shanghai were the most promising, Amoy because of its fine natural harbour and its accessibility to the tea farms, Shanghai because of the glittering prospect of tapping the trade of the Yangtze. But the abuses were worse than ever: the customs frauds, the squeeze imposed by Chinese officials, above all the opium trade and the traffic in coolies. A description written by the British consul at Shanghai in 1844 matches almost word for word what the American missionary, Elijah Bridgman, had reported of Canton in 1840. The consul wrote: 'All boats laden with opium daily and unhesitatingly pass the Custom house boats unchecked and unexamined. . . . I have ascertained that the highest Chinese officers of this place were acquainted with the transshipment of the opium before I obtained information, and yet no notice was taken and no measures were adopted by them.'[11]

The five per cent treaty tariff anticipated a utopian open door for all Western traders whose governments took advantage of the most-favoured-nation pledge; but since the Chinese customs service remained unreformed and as corrupt as ever, the foreign merchants continued the traditional practice of competitive deals with venal bureaucrats. Smuggling and fraudulent declarations were so common and so open that to condemn them as 'illegal' was merely to arouse contempt for the paper treaty system. Then in 1851, with the outbreak of the Taiping rebellion – a spontaneous revolution among the masses of the interior, maddened by floods and famines and burning with hatred of the Manchu régime – the treaty system faced collapse. The Taipings moved down the Yangtze, capturing Nanking and threatening Shanghai.

The determined British consul Rutherford Alcock, who had already taken steps to secure the foreign settlement at Shanghai, compelled British merchants to give written guarantees that they would pay the duties they owed as soon as an agency capable of receiving payment could be created. Somewhat reluctantly Humphrey Marshall, Alcock's American colleague, agreed to take similar action. Merchants of both nationalities were ready to trade with either the rebels or the mandarins, but Alcock and Marshall sided with the latter. Under a British inspector a model customs house was created at Shanghai, receiving payments from the foreign merchants at the uniform rates and making remittances to the imperial court at Peking. This was the origin of the Inspectorate of Maritime Customs, backed by Sir John Bowring and extended during the next few years to the other treaty ports. It salvaged the otherwise unworkable treaty system, and in 1861 the imperial government accepted it and put it under the jurisdiction of the *tsungli yamen*, the newly created Chinese ministry of foreign affairs.

The Inspectorate was in the tradition of China: a joint administration of Chinese and barbarians. The British and Americans controlled the Inspectorate, and were supported by a staff of Chinese which expanded numerically as the volume of business increased. Under Robert Hart, who was Inspector-General for nearly half a century, the Inspectorate earned a unique reputation for honesty and efficiency, an independent agency headed by foreigners but not under foreign control. With Hart and his associates collaborating intimately with the *tsungli yamen* and absorbing the Chinese point of view, a certain amount of cultural assimilation took place.

The impatience of merchants and missionaries, frustrated on the one hand by Chinese xenophobia but stimulated on the other by growing opportunities for trade and religion, was matched by the vexation of foreign governments, especially the British, over Chinese intransigence. Nothing short of complete surrender to the Western system of international relations would satisfy the British, French, American and Russian governments. (Russia was by now, like the Mongols of past centuries, beginning to press on China from north of the Great Wall.) At Canton the viceroy, Yeh Ming-ch'en, stood unmoved by Anglo-French attacks which were renewed in 1856 in reprisal for minor offences committed by the Chinese. An American and a Russian plenipotentiary arrived at Macao, prepared to share in the fruits of the expected Chinese capitulation. They are 'living with me here cheek by jowl', reported Paul Forbes, 'and draw together socially as well as politically.' The report is tantalizing because we have no other information on this interesting personal and semi-official relationship. The friendship, we know, continued since both envoys sailed north to Tientsin on the same ship in advance of the Anglo-French expeditionary force. Yeh Ming-ch'en, in Forbes's eyes, was a 'plucky old fellow' seeking martyrdom and determined 'to keep out the foreigner or die or else live only as the impersonation of the Chinese policy of exclusion'. He seems to have had his way, for the British exiled him to India.

In terms of trade Shanghai was the great goal, and the Americans were as eager as the British to push up the river. Forbes compared the opening-up of the city with the contemporaneous American expedition against Japan. 'The fact is,' he told his wife, 'this is getting to be the most interesting point of the world. Great events are in embryo, and what with the Rebellion in China threatening to overturn the present Dynasty and that long sealed country Japan on the eve of being opened', he felt unable to tear himself away and go home. Alcock and the new and very co-operative American consul, Robert Murphy, were working with the local *tao-tai* (administrative official) in Shanghai in setting up land regulations permitting the foreigners to rent land, reside permanently and govern themselves autonomously outside the walled native city. Russell and Company, Jardine-Mathieson, Dent and other British firms were already on the ground and doing business. This was the start of the International Settlement, a unique enclave of foreign nationals who were self-governing and independent of their respective home governments. The International Settlement and the Inspectorate of Maritime Customs were conceived and implemented by the same four men – Rutherford Alcock in particular, but also Sir John Bowring and the two Americans, Robert Murphy and Robert McLane, who followed the somewhat sour Humphrey Marshall as United States commissioner.

The missionaries too were pleased with the turn of events, reporting to the American Board in Boston in 1859 that their work would go faster now that the northern ports were open. The Anglo-French converged in force upon Tientsin in 1858, and when the emperor still refused to grant them admittance to Peking they brought up

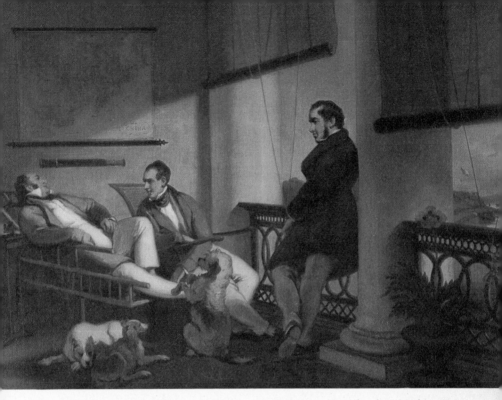

13 This painting by Chinnery (Macao, 1842) shows members of Jardine, Mathieson and Company and Russell and Company (both seated).

additional forces and drove their way into the city. For China the experience of yielding recognition at the cannon's mouth was costly and painful: eleven new treaty ports were forced open, the unlimited right to travel into the interior was granted to foreigners under the protection of extraterritoriality; a war indemnity was imposed, and a permanent wound inflicted by the plundering and burning of the emperor's summer palace, whose splendours the conquerors themselves 'found it difficult to describe'. During these triumphs and tragedies, relentlessly carried through by the British and French, the Americans and Russians stood by as friendly onlookers. William B. Reed, the American envoy, helped with the negotiations and expressed his gratitude for the assistance rendered by his secretary of legation, Dr S. Wells Williams, and by his interpreter, the Reverend W. A. P. Martin.

'Progress' had been accomplished. Commerce and the Christian religion were mutual beneficiaries.

3 The United States steps forward in Japan

The historical stage for the Western advent in Japan need not be set so far back as is necessary in the case of China. The seventeenth century, or at the most three hundred years, seems long enough. But there are sharp contrasts all along the way. For instance, in the case of China, American private enterprise took the initiative in 1784 and held it for many years. Merchants and missionaries began it and kept pace with their British competitors; but, in spite of the very large American stake in the China trade, the government was for at least half a century a minus quantity. A cruising naval squadron put in an appearance in the early 1820s, assuming its share of the burden in the suppression of piracy. Obviously, however, the cliché that 'trade follows the flag' has no validity for China. Spurred by mercantile interests, the government in 1832 sent out a diplomatic mission; but, like Lord Amherst's attempt in 1816 to get to Peking, it was abortive. Even the successful diplomacy of Caleb Cushing, consummated by his treaty with Ch'i-ying in 1844, cannot be valued very highly: the American China merchants do not seem to have been impressed by it, and in any event they would have obtained the same privileges as the British even if Cushing had never appeared on the scene. And as late as the Second Anglo-China War and its success in coercing the Chinese into surrender, the American government had no policy and took no real initiative. It was a 'neutral', ready enough, however, to snatch at whatever advantages came its way as a result of the Anglo-French aggressions.

In the case of Japan the exact opposite was true. There the United States government seized the initiative. From the very outset it had a policy, formulated and set down in the positive language of the instructions given to Commodore Matthew Calbraith Perry in 1852. There was no American mercantile community in Japan at the time or for some years thereafter. A number of American mariners, notably whalers hunting their prey in the Sea of Okhotsk, needed to replenish their provisions and water supply by means of temporary visits to the northern islands of Japan. But by comparison the stake was small, and while doubtless the need was great it does not by itself adequately explain the elaborate steps taken by the government, first through the navy and then by diplomacy, to open Japan.

Other contrasts with China are significant. An island archipelago in relation to the Asiatic mainland (similar to the British Isles in relation to Europe, but with 120 miles between the nearest points instead of the twenty-one across the Straits of Dover), Japan enjoyed a natural protection from foreigners not possible for the Chinese. Until the middle of the nineteenth century the Japanese were neither tempted to venture abroad themselves nor exposed to invasion by others. The one potential enemy, China, entertained no naval ambitions except for the brief period 1405-24 when, as we have seen, Chinese fleets established temporary dominance over the Indian Ocean. An agricultural country with a few cities prospering on internal trade, Japan remained unmolested.

Again by comparison with its huge neighbour Japan did not, and could not, enjoy the delusion that it was itself the centre of the world. Unlike the Chinese, the Japanese were not 'barbarian-tamers'; and though persistently hostile to foreigners, they could not afford the luxury of a self-centred doctrine of superiority. China was a unique culture, a civilization which recognized no equals; Japan was a developing nation, with institutions and *mores* approximating to those of the dynastic states of Western Europe. During the twelfth century internal feudal warfare culminated in a military administration, the Bakufu, gaining the upper hand and setting up its capital at Yedo (Tokyo). The Bakufu, familiarly described by Western writers as the shogunate, preserved and respected the hereditary dynasty at Kyoto, but effectively put itself between the emperor and the *daimyo* (feudal lords). These were obliged to leave hostages (children or wives) for their good behaviour at the court of the shogun, and were permitted no intercourse with the throne save through the medium of the shogun's representative at Kyoto. The shogunate itself became hereditary, and in the seventeenth century under the Tokugawa family it matured into a powerful absolutism which maintained itself until past the middle of the nineteenth. In other words, there is a remarkable parallel both institutionally and in point of time between Japan and the so-called 'divine right' monarchies of Western Europe, the principal difference being that in the case of Japan the shogun exercised the sovereign authority in the name of the emperor. The latter remained remote and aloof, a deity or son of heaven in the Chinese sense, but with none of the power of the Chinese emperor or of the active monarchs of Western Europe.

Ieyasu, the first of the ruling Tokugawas, set the standards which endured from the time of his death in 1616 (the year of Shakespeare's demise in far-away England) until cracks appeared two hundred years later which were too wide to be papered over. The régime was

14 The arrival of Commodore Perry's 'black ships' off Uraga, 8 July 1853.

non-religious, but the rules it lived by read like the strict moral code of the New England Puritans. 'Human life,' declares one of these rules, attributed to Ieyasu himself, 'is like going on a long journey carrying a heavy load. You will not be disappointed if you think that hardship is the common lot. When desires arise in your heart think back to times when you suffered distress.'[1] Shakespearian tragedy is here, unrelieved by the touch of gaiety and humour. The régime aimed at safeguarding the *status quo*, a feudal order wherein every man had his place subject to the will of the shogun – the *daimyo* having their respective quotas of samurai, or warrior-retainers, on call from Yedo. Corrupting influences, especially the alien Christian religion with its implied threat of foreign political encroachment, were barred. Portuguese and Spanish Jesuits had inspired Ieyasu with such fear that he expelled them and decreed death for any European caught landing on Japanese shores. And the success of the Bakufu in suppressing an internal insurrection in 1637 marked the point at which Ieyasu's programme of seclusion demonstrated its greatest efficiency. Only a handful of Dutch traders was allowed to remain, bottled up on the small island of Deshima in Nagasaki Bay where they could be watched. Unlike other Europeans, the Dutch kept religion out of business, though even in their private worship they had to be careful.

Possibly ancient Sparta furnishes the only other example of a martial state keeping entirely to itself. For two centuries the Bakufu remained on guard, but subversive influences and threatening gestures had their cumulative effect. Apart from the impossibility of an unbroken chain of resolute rulers, peace had its perils. The neat feudal structure envisaged by Ieyasu could not be kept intact. Without war the samurai could not be kept under Spartan discipline. Restless, maladjusted youth – *rōnin* – were part of the social scene even in Ieyasu's time, their numbers tending to grow at an average of five thousand per year and estimated to total 400,000 by 1850. Some of the *rōnin* solved their own problems, making good farmers or tradespeople or even developing literary and artistic abilities. But, rudderless and having no real place in society, the *rōnin* were thorns in the flesh of the latter-day shoguns, a lawless element open to hire for deeds of violence and gang warfare. The shogun Yoshimune, who died in 1751, was the last of the Bakufu rulers strong enough to restrain this and other corrupting forces, such as extravagance and misgovernment, working toward the eventual downfall of the régime. Like its mainland contemporary, the Ch'ing dynasty, the Tokugawa shogunate took the downward path from about 1750.

Forced idleness and poverty were the lot of the samurai as a class and even of some of the *daimyo* at the turn of the century. Only shreds of the feudal system remained. The Bakufu itself was now operating on deficit financing, going into debt to merchant bankers and resorting to sundry schemes of currency manipulation. The emergence of an urban middle class, in part the effect of the luxurious tastes of the *daimyo* for things that could be made and sold only in cities, called for a shift from a barter to a money economy not suited to a feudal society. Chronic failures in the rice crop, price changes and a tax squeeze felt most directly by the peasants led to an explosive situation by the middle of the nineteenth century. A well-meaning but futile attempt at reform instituted by the shogun's chief minister in 1841 only served to advertise the weakness of the Bakufu.

In about 1808 Russian vessels from Kamchatka and British vessels from the Indian Ocean gave the Bakufu another reason for feeling anxious. In 1825 it actually issued an unenforceable order to destroy any foreign ship entering Japanese coastal waters, but intelligence of the easy British victories over China in the Opium War put an end to this policy. Appeasement of foreigners henceforth became the rule, marked by the polite treatment accorded a British naval vessel in Nagasaki harbour in 1845. Food, water and fuel were made available, but the foreigners were asked to go away and not try to land their crews on Japanese soil.

Fears of foreign aggression became an obsession, however, as marked by the writings of two authors, Takashima Shūhan and Sakuma Shōzan, who advised sudden and drastic military reforms in order to meet the expected attack. These men aroused heated argument among ultra-conservative traditionalists, but the later founders of the modern Japanese army and navy found inspiration in their writings. A few writers, notably Yokoi Shōnan, a contemporary of Satsuma, drew on their imaginations to depict a new Japan rivalling the imperial powers and conquering China as the first step in the direction of its own 'destiny'. Shōnan's ideas were anathema to the anti-foreign party – he and Satsuma were later assassinated. But when in 1853 Commodore Perry forced the Bakufu to make a decision, Shōnan counselled moderation and declared his belief that the time had come to abandon the exclusion policy and deal with the foreign powers on their terms.

With the Americans following the British so closely in China, it was to be expected that the United States would make the decisive move against Japan. 'Like a huge breakwater,' as one observer put it, 'Japan stretches along the coast of Asia, and receives the first shock of the Pacific billows.'[2] The island kingdom once opened, the United States could be sure of its own trade route to the Orient. Japan would offset the advantages which the British derived from Singapore and Hongkong. Commodore Perry said as much, for he had a sharp eye for the naval strategy of the Pacific. Daniel Webster, still Secretary of State when Perry was chosen, restated Thomas Jefferson's thesis of 'the North American road to India'. Webster could hardly be uninterested in the China trade: he was a citizen of Massachusetts, and his own home town, Newburyport, had China connections. Now that the United States had deprived Mexico of California, Massachusetts and New York entrepreneurs were beginning to show an interest in a transcontinental railway. Japan, asserted Webster, was 'the last link in that great chain, which unites all the world, by the early establishment of a line of steamers from California to China'.[3] Prerequisite to this ambition was a railway to the Pacific coast.

By this time there was ground for believing that the future of the China trade lay more to the north of the Yangtze. Shanghai was attracting mercantile interest – Paul Forbes, as we have seen, was confident of this, and he perceived the connection between Japan and this promising new treaty port. By 1849 the International Settlement was a going concern, and two years later a start was made with the Inspectorate of Maritime Customs. China, moreover, was expected to yield more treaty ports, all north of the Yangtze.

'Christian civilization and commerce has [*sic*] closed upon the Japanese Empire on both sides. It lies between the faces of the two great commercial millstones of the world.'[4] A writer in an American church magazine pointed out that Yedo and San Francisco were almost on the same parallel of north latitude, 36°. Moreover, American religious and commercial influence was now dominant in the Sandwich Islands – Webster in 1842 had in effect declared the islands an American sphere of influence; and in 1854, the year in which Perry 'opened' Japan, the Pierce administration made a calculated attempt (which was abortive) to annex them.

Japan *per se* was not valued highly for the trade that it would yield. The China merchants dismissed it for its poverty in contrast to China's great wealth; and, in drawing up its instructions for Perry, the State Department put trade at the bottom of the list of what it wanted. No particular treaty ports were designated. Food, water and fuel (including coal) for American vessels, especially whaling ships, operating in the Sea of Okhotsk were stressed. Out of touch with even the Hawaiian Islands, whalers needed supplies and sometimes the chance for landing and careening their vessels. Perry himself had been to New Bedford, Massachusetts, the home of the whaling interests, and had learned at first hand of their needs, notably from Captain Joseph C. Delano (another Delano!). The American government thus had practical motives for levying demands upon Japan. But these were not the controlling motives, and it seems likely that they did not weigh heavily in the scale of Perry's own values. Japan was a staging-point on the route to Shanghai and North China, vital to the American commercial empire in the North Pacific.

Glory for its own sake was a factor. Perry had only accepted the assignment after satisfying himself of the prestige it would bring to the country as well as to himself. He was a prominent career commander in the navy, with an enviable reputation gained in the war with Mexico; and in 1852 his own choice for his next command was the Mediterranean squadron. But study of the prospects in the Pacific

15 *The Procession of Western Nationalities in Tokyo.*
Woodcut by
the Japanese artist Sadahide.

convinced him otherwise. He was a zealous believer in the 'destiny' of the United States, desirous of pushing beyond the already immense annexations at the expense of Mexico, of building and dominating an isthmian canal across Central America, and of outstripping Britain.

S. Wells Williams, the devout missionary whom Perry picked up in Hongkong to serve as his interpreter and to whom he probably confided his intentions, understood what it was all about. Privileges for whaling vessels, Williams declared, 'are our ostensible reasons for going to this great outlay and sending this powerful squadron to Japanese waters; the real reasons are glorification of the Yankee nation, and food for praising ourselves'. But Williams was the true missionary, considering the Japanese just as important as the Chinese in fulfilling 'God's purposes'. 'I have a full conviction,' he wrote, 'that the seclusion policy of the nations of Eastern Asia is not according to God's plan of mercy to these peoples, and their govern-

16 *An American Merchant and his Daughter in Tokyo.* Japanese coloured woodblock print, second half of the nineteenth century.

ment must change through fear or force, that the people may be free.'[5]

Williams's reference to the 'powerful squadron' was exaggerated even for those times: at its entry into the Bay of Yedo it consisted of two coal-burning paddle steamers, one sloop of war and one supply ship. To the Japanese they were 'black ships' (*kurofine*), the designation for all foreign vessels, and they drew up in line-of-battle as they anchored. The Commodore had the authority to use force, should persuasion fail, but he was too masterful a man and too confident that the Japanese would get the point before resorting to hasty action. The Bakufu had the lesson of China to reflect upon, the Dutch at Nagasaki had warned it, and foreign warships – British, Russian, American – had hovered off the Japanese coast.

Perry had sailed east from the United States, crossing the Indian Ocean and enduring a long, forced stay at Hongkong and then a

47

17 *Landing of Commodore Perry and Men of the Squadron, to meet the Imperial Commissioners at Yoku-Hama, Japan, March 8, 1854.* Watercolour by William Heine.

fortnight at Shanghai, where Russell and Company lavished the officers with hospitality. At Hongkong he took on board two young men of note who were later to contribute to the fame of the expedition. They were Bayard Taylor, who had already earned a reputation for his writings, and William Heine, an artist whose paintings and sketches left a fine pictorial record of the expedition. Heine played up to the Commodore's ego by placing him in the centre of the picture of the landing scene without regard to the rules of perspective. Young Bayard Taylor's enthusiasm was infectious. He had only a master's mate's rating, but 'I belong to the great American Navy – that glorious institution which scatters civilization with every broadside and illuminates the dark places of the earth with the light of its rockets and bombshells'.[6] Both Taylor and Heine subsequently wrote books on the voyage. But the man who indubitably knew more about the inside of Japan than any other foreigner of the time had been turned down by Perry. He was Philipp von Siebold, a German naturalist who had lived and taught at the shogun's court. Perry surmised he was in Russian pay, and he may have been right. Von Siebold joined the Russian squadron which followed Perry into Yedo Bay, and later 'punished' Perry by giving the Russian admiral credit for the first success in Japan.

Japanese guardboats surrounded Perry's four ships when the squadron anchored off Uraga on 8 July 1853, and some 17,000 men were mobilized to do duty along the shores of the bay, yet no hostilities ensued. The internal weakness and indecision previously described in

this chapter paralysed the Bakufu; it dared not risk a showdown, though the drama of the confrontation is preserved in the watercolours of William Heine. Considering the audacity of Perry's manœuvres during his eight-day stay, the absence of trouble with his unwilling hosts seems astounding. Under his orders, his men methodically went about their task of making soundings in the harbour and charting the shorelines, always watched but never attacked by the Japanese guardboats. When one American survey boat rowed deep into the inner bay and found itself surrounded by forty-five Japanese boats, the tension did almost snap. Pageantry and strict military discipline on both sides marked Perry's landing and meeting with high-ranking Japanese officials. The Commodore succeeded in formally delivering to them a letter from the President to the emperor, but that was all. Actually it was quite a bit. They were 'very intractable people', upon whom 'I found it necessary to practise a very novel system of diplomacy'. In about a year, he informed them, he would return for an answer bringing stronger forces.

The second trip proved easier than perhaps Perry expected. 'Old Sly Boots' – a nickname among his crew – did not intend to let the Russians, British or French get a start on him, so he appeared again at Uraga in February 1854. The Bakufu was now reconciled to making minimum concessions, and it agreed to a treaty opening Shimoda and Hakodate for supply of 'wood, water, provisions and coal, and other articles their necessities may require'. Located near the entrance to the Bay of Yedo, but isolated by a mountain range,

Shimoda was satisfactory for the limited purposes specified, but for no other. Hakodate, on the northern island of Hokkaido, lay near the path of whaling ships hunting in the North Pacific and was ideal for the safety of castaways and for the supply of provisions. But these towns were not treaty ports, nor was it intended that they should be.

Perry wanted the Bonin Islands annexed – they were unoccupied at the time – and considering their excellent location and the appetite of the American government for strategic islands, its indifference to his proposal seems incomprehensible. Party politics supplies part of the answer: the Democratic administration studiously avoided giving Perry, a Whig, any recognition until its hand was forced. Moreover, it was meeting with reversals in its current attempts to annex Cuba and Hawaii and to get the upper hand in Central America, nor were its hopes of quieting the internal controversy over slavery in the territories being realized. So a valuable acquisition that might have been accomplished in more auspicious times went by the board.

Contemporary with Perry's voyage was the United States Surveying Expedition to the North Pacific, which remained out until 1856 under the command of Lieutenant John Rodgers. Even more candidly than Perry, Rodgers expressed optimism that the United States, once having developed a route from San Francisco to Shanghai, would secure a stranglehold on the China trade. 'I think that the Pacific Railroad, and steamers to China, will turn the tide of commerce this way,' he declared. 'We shall carry to Europe their teas and silks from New York. . . . The results are so vast as to dazzle sober calculation.'[7] But the reception that Rodgers got when he called at Hakodate for food and water was not flattering; and as with Perry the administration at home was unresponsive.

Perry in his treaty had extracted from the Japanese the right to open a consulate at Shimoda; and Congress, in passing an act to remodel the diplomatic and consular system of the government, provided for such a post. After some delay the appointment went to Townsend Harris, a Democrat and a China merchant of New York City. Only after the chamber of commerce of that city had put on a celebration in Perry's honour did the administration in Washington give him his due, and it may have been pressure from the same source that induced the administration to proceed with the consulate. At any rate, the prominent Whig senator William Henry Seward, known to be an outspoken advocate of pressing forward into Asia, used his influence in conjunction with Perry to get Harris the job; and the Secretary of State, William L. Marcy, a former Governor of

New York, took up the cause. Marcy was well aware that the Japanese preferred seclusion, but he told Harris to push for the privileges of treaty ports. In other words, a new interest in trade with Japan was now manifest, and the latter was not to be allowed to refuse. If it did, Harris was to tell the Japanese officials, 'we will be sure to demand, in a way which they cannot resist, privileges which we are entitled to'.[8]

Harris scrupulously abstained from unveiling this threat; and since the warship that carried him to Shimoda promptly departed, not to return, Harris himself must have felt its futility. Moreover, he remained completely alone in this small alien community, save for a Dutchman whom he took on as his interpreter, and he was unable to communicate with Washington, D.C. Being a strict sabbatarian, he repeatedly refused to see anyone on Sunday, and on other days when officials from the Bakufu came to talk with him, he felt 'like a horse in a mill' covering the same ground over and over again. He would not go away, as they requested; but his own feeling toward them is betrayed in his journal by the frequent recurrence of such nouns as 'cunning', 'falsehood' and 'mendacity'. 'I am only nine days distant from Hongkong,' he wrote plaintively, 'yet I am more isolated than any American official in any part of the world.'[9]

But Harris felt the Japanese people in general to be well disposed and inclined to open the country, and even the officials, he noted, were daily becoming more friendly. In June 1857 came his first break: the shogun signed a convention opening Nagasaki to American vessels needing repairs, water and provisions and even coal, granting American citizens the right to reside permanently in Shimoda and Hakodate, and conceding extraterritoriality. In July of the following year the Japanese went all the way with a treaty of amity and commerce: the United States was to have a diplomatic mission at Yedo and consulates, if it chose, at five new treaty ports, including Yokohama which was much better located for trade than Shimoda; and if Japan had trouble with any other foreign power, the United States might play the role of 'friendly mediator'. Clearly Harris intended the United States to be the leader in Japan, in contrast to the secondary role it was playing in China; and as for the Japanese, the tragedy of China in its second war with Britain (joined by France) was all too apparent. Japan could gamble no longer on its prized seclusion. While China was suffering from further humiliation, with the British and French forcing their way into Peking and burning the emperor's magnificent summer palace, the Japanese in 1860 on their own initiative sent a diplomatic mission to the United States. Obviously Japan was learning the lesson of contemporary history.

But naturally the lesson came hard. Adjustment to a new order, in which foreigners were at liberty to travel in the country, buy property and live near sacred shrines, and all the while be exempt from local laws, was a big undertaking for a society which had survived two centuries in successful seclusion. Perry and then Harris were greeted with dismay at a time when native society was beset with internal tensions and rendered apprehensive by the spectacle of the commotions in China. From a more distant standpoint the mendacity of the shogun's envoys in their talks with Harris is understandable. A few of the wiser heads at the shogun's court, notably Lords Ii and Hotta, realized there was no choice but to bow to necessity; but xenophobia mingled with enmity toward the Bakufu, which, as we have seen, was already in straits, made a deliberate decision difficult. The outlying *daimyo* and the recluse-like court nobles at Kyoto constituted a powerful diehard party. Sir George Sansom has made use of a telling simile from a Japanese historian to drive home the scene: 'Opinion in Japan at this time was like a great whirlpool formed by a confusion of many smaller whirlpools.' [10]

The confusion rose to a climax in 1863 when the shogun issued an order, conveyed to the foreign envoys in Yedo, that from June 24 all foreigners were to leave the country and the ports were to be closed. But along with the formal order went the assurance that nothing would be done to enforce it. The order emanated from Kyoto, whither the shogun had gone breaking a precedent of two centuries. There followed an insurrection by two clans, the Choshu and the Satsuma, accompanied by assassinations and attacks on foreigners, but it was crushed by retaliatory action by British, French, Dutch and American warships. An attempted action on the part of the Bakufu served only to advertise its weakness. The coincidental death of the incumbent shogun and the enthronement of a new emperor who took the name of Meiji concluded this extraordinary transition. The rebel clans fell in line behind the emperor, the Bakufu met with an ignominious end, and the foreign powers secured from the throne an acknowledgment of the rights previously conceded them by the shogun. Internal tension, punctuated by sporadic outbreaks of xenophobia and personal assaults on foreigners, continued; and the foreign powers exacerbated the situation by refusing to relinquish their extraterritorial rights in favour of the new régime. But with the Meiji restoration in 1868 Japan entered a new era.

4 'Antiforeignism' in China, the 'Yellow Peril' in America

'Steam is a great civilizer,' wrote Samuel Wells Williams, the now famous missionary, to William Henry Seward, the Secretary of State, in 1868, 'and if its power can be used to bring the people of this land into better acquaintance with each other, it will tend to the maintenance of peace, security of travel, and prosperity and strength of every department of government. For these and other reasons I regard the extension of steam navigation in China as fraught with many advantages.'[1]

No doubt Williams knew of the success Russell and Company was having with its steamboat business on the Yangtze. Drawing on its past earnings, the American firm had set up a subsidiary, the Shanghai Steam Navigation Company; and, with Paul Forbes and Edward Cunningham as managers, this company had forged to first place in the profitable carrying trade between Shanghai and Hankow. Forbes had secured the best waterfront sites at the new river treaty ports, and Cunningham, who as consul at Shanghai had collaborated with Rutherford Alcock, was gifted in promoting good relations with Chinese merchants.

Four or five of the company's steamers plied the six-hundred-mile run on a regular schedule, including calls at the intermediate ports of Chinkiang and Kiukang; and for about the five years from 1867 to 1872 it held a virtual monopoly of this trade, together with a dominant place in the coastal business from Shanghai south to Ningpo and north to Tientsin. At the end of this period two British firms, the China Navigation Company and the China Coast Navigation Company – the latter a subsidiary of Jardine-Mathieson – entered the competition and the American firm, finding itself unable to keep up the pace, submitted to a pooling agreement proposed by the first and more aggressive of the British companies. Cunningham had meanwhile given up and returned to Boston, but not before expressing a sentiment that seems to have been common among the British-American business community in Shanghai. 'We are, in truth,' he had written in a private letter in 1869, 'all cosmopolitans, more perhaps than most of us know. . . . If there is any struggle at all, past or to come, for the steam carrying business in China, it is not between different foreigners but between foreigners and Chinese. . . .

Heaven save us all, I say, from Chinese owned and managed steamboats.'[2]

Cunningham, Forbes and their British competitors knew Chinese merchants. But, though there were exceptions like the Houquas of Canton, the merchants were sharply differentiated from the mandarins – the *shih*, or scholar-bureaucrats, who were the traditional ruling class of China. Western ideas of 'progress' struck no responsive chord among the mandarins who, as disciples of Confucius, treated society from the emperor down in terms of fixed relationships. As we have already noticed, every good Chinese performed the kotow – as a mark of respect, but not of servility as Occidentals wrongheadedly believed. Most honoured and influential among the mandarins were the literati, those few who had qualified in the traditional examinations which in the passage of time had stagnated.

Better than the merchants, but still basically unsympathetic, Williams and his younger fellow missionary, W. A. P. Martin, developed respect for and some comprehension of the meaning of Chinese culture. Williams grasped the frustrations that lay ahead: under the treaties of 1858 the interior of China lay open to foreigners to travel for pleasure or on business, to establish residence and secure title to property, and to propagate the Christian religion. The Shanghai Chamber of Commerce, for instance, expected to treat the whole of China as 'one vast treaty port' open to limitless exploitation; and the French, lagging far behind the Anglo-Americans in commercial success, had gratified their national ego through the religious privileges they had extracted. While the government of Napoleon III intended these privileges for the Roman Catholic Church, the eighty or more American Protestant missionaries in China at the time stood to share in the benefits; like the Shanghai businessmen they conceived of China as completely open, and they represented to their home churches in America the unlimited opportunities for evangelization among 'the heathen'.

Williams and Martin, being close to the imperial government in Peking, appreciated the need for patience: the Chinese had much to learn concerning the legal duties and inevitable changes the Christian nations had in store for them. The people of the interior feared steamboats, railways, machinery and the telegraph, and amidst all the pressures bearing down upon them there was a question mark over the future integrity of the empire. Williams commented on the expanding opium trade – 88,000 chests imported in the single year 1867 – and he sent Seward the text of a secret memorial written by

18 The Seventh Prince on board the steamboat of the China Merchants' Steam Navigation Company. Chinese woodcut, second half of the nineteenth century.

Tseng Kuo-fan, the victor over the Taiping in 1864 and now highest in rank among the provincial governors-general. Tseng Kuo-fan was one of the 'new officials' at Peking – men who realized that the Chinese had no choice but to learn how to meet the West. Steamboat traffic on the Yangtze had driven hundreds of boatmen to desperation, and more 'improvements' foisted on the population might develop into a calamity. Building a railway in this crowded country, added Williams, was quite different from building one in the United States.

Still, Williams was pleased with the progress evidenced at the top. A new bureau, the *tsungli yamen*, had been created in 1861 to deal with the treaty powers, and Prince Kung, another of the 'new officials', was in charge of it and in close touch with Sir Robert Hart, the Inspector-General of Maritime Customs. William Martin, originally a Presbyterian missionary, had turned his attention to international law, first translating an American treatise on the subject and then in 1868 himself teaching it in Chinese at the Tungwen Kuan, a new institution authorized by the emperor to acquaint officials with Western concepts.

Both Williams and Martin conferred often with Hart and with the British minister, Sir Rutherford Alcock, who had been promoted from the consulate at Shanghai; and Martin subsequently paid tribute to Hart for doing more than any other man to save China from destruction at the hands of the treaty powers. Under his supervision the Inspectorate earned a reputation for integrity and efficiency. Neither Hart nor Alcock believed in the mercantile-missionary dream of China as one vast treaty port; and at their urging the British government dissociated itself after 1861 from the ambitions of 'old China hands' like Jardine, Mathieson and Company.

Through Wells Williams, Anson Burlingame, the new envoy whom Secretary Seward had sent out from Washington, befriended Hart and earned his respect. Burlingame recognized the value of the Inspectorate and agreed on a policy of restraint in asking for concessions. The *yamen* was urged to establish diplomatic missions abroad, and at Hart's suggestion it commissioned Burlingame to visit the capitals of the treaty powers on its behalf. Hart and Alcock liked Burlingame's direct manner, but they tried to blur the romantic picture of China that had caught his fancy. A natural-born enthusiast, Burlingame knew little of the country outside the walls of Peking.

Upon his return to Washington in 1868, he negotiated a treaty under which the United States and China 'cordially recognize the inherent and inalienable right of man to change his home and allegiance'. The United States had been receiving immigrants from Europe on this basis ever since the Revolution, and at this very time it was on the verge of inducing the British government to relinquish by treaty its immemorial, but unenforceable, rule of the indefeasible allegiance of its subjects. Thousands of Chinese immigrants had been flocking into the western American states ever since 1850, but the high-sounding phrases of the Burlingame treaty were remote from the realities of the harsh reception they got in California. Williams was aware of this animosity at the popular level, and he observed that if Americans in China had suffered one tithe of the wrongs the Chinese in America had endured during the preceding dozen years, the American government would have made it a cause for war.

Devoutly religious men, Williams and Martin blamed the many disturbances they witnessed in China upon the shock which the foreign steamboat traffic administered to the native boatmen. They were so committed to evangelizing the Chinese masses that they appear never to have realized how offensive the alien Christian religion was, especially to the mandarins. Nor were they aware that the imperial government had not informed the provincial governors of the religious privileges under the treaties, lest the intelligence provoke a rebellion. The missionaries were 'prisoners of their own limited motive', an effective phrase coined by Victor Purcell, one of the leading students of Chinese 'antiforeignism'.

Rationalism, scepticism and this-worldliness were native characteristics of Confucian China, readily understandable to the non-religious, philosophical schools of thought in the West but not to orthodox Christians, Catholic or Protestant. Coincidentally Darwin's *The Origin of Species* appeared as a challenge to Christian theology at the very time (1859) that Christendom was getting into position for its greatest assault on Chinese philosophy. As messengers of Christ, the missionaries defined their role as exponents of the superior civilization of the West, including its capitalist economy. But from time immemorial Confucian China had conditioned itself to be the centre and teacher of civilization; and as a system of ethics it rejected what the Western missionary took for granted – the alliance with business.

This basic ideological incompatibility was brought into the realm of practical conflict during the second half of the nineteenth century: first, the Taiping rebellion, while threatening China with an appalling breakdown, boasted of Christian influence; and then the arrival of the missionaries in ever-increasing numbers after 1860 gave the mandarins serious cause for antagonism. A good illustration of this mutual hostility is the reception accorded to a violently anti-Christian Chinese book, first published in 1861 and translated under the title *Death Blow to Corrupt Doctrines*. The American Board missionaries in Peking reported it as 'an abominable book recently issued by the literary class against Christianity and widely circulated in several provinces . . . filled with loathsome obscenity and the grossest misrepresentations and falsehoods'. More calmly, Sir Robert Hart thought it 'very clever and . . . a queer mixture of truth and error . . . evidently the work of a well-read man, and I have no doubt but that the literati have it, and many more like it, on their shelves'.[3]

For the time being American Protestants confined themselves to the treaty ports, but French Catholics took to the interior provinces in numbers. In provinces like Szechuan, Kiangsu, Chihli and Fukien they formed the advance guard of foreign intruders, confronting a village population unprepared for the revolutionary changes that these barbarians from the unknown outside world meant to impose upon it. In various ways the missionaries managed to antagonize the population at all levels, and most of all the provincial mandarins who easily recognized that their own position was being jeopardized.

Traditionally the provincial governors and their subordinates were free from interference by Peking, although they could be recalled and punished upon occasion.

In 1861 Kweichow province was in the hands of T'ien Hsing-shu, a reckless young soldier who made no secret of his detestation of Christianity and of the foreigner who carried its banner. T'ien was already in the bad books of Peking for other reasons, but the pompous exhibition put on by a French bishop under cover of his treaty rights brought a swift reprisal in the form of attacks on his cathedral and a convent. This incident set the standard for the recurrent riots that ensued throughout the provinces and culminated in a massacre in Tientsin in 1870. Examination periods in cities like Nanking, where sixty thousand students were expected to congregate, were particularly dangerous for missionaries, who knew in advance what to expect. 'Our houses are but a short distance from the place where they will meet,' reported an English female missionary in 1869, but 'the Lord can keep us. We are in His hands, and it is a joy to know it.'[4]

Such self-invited martyrdom, familiar enough in the history of religions like Christianity and Buddhism, meant endless trouble and embarrassment for the foreign representatives in Peking, who were expected to force the Chinese to live up to their treaty obligations. Missionaries constituted a fifth column in China, undermining local government in the provinces and pitting the central government against its own populace on the one hand and against the treaty powers on the other. Since they penetrated more deeply into Chinese society, rocking the foundations wherever they went, these well-meaning but uncompromising people did more than their share in raising the temperature of xenophobia to fever heat.

Fortunately the British government, once having obtained the favours its merchants demanded, decided to relax its attitude and take the advice of its representatives in China. The new policy of moderation, which involved rejection of special requests for gunboats, coincided with the growth of anti-clerical and anti-imperial sentiment at home. Conscious too of its dilemma in India, the British government grew wary of being sucked into the internal affairs of China.

'Missionaries are people who are always provoking the men of the world', remarked The Times sententiously, and the London Missionary Society advised its field workers in China to keep to the ports. French anti-clericalism also had its cumulative effects, and the government of Napoleon III, originally so zealous in promoting privileges for the Roman Catholic Church, soon discovered itself out of its depth in China. The bishop who caused the outbreak in Kweichow in 1861 got a sharp reproof from the French chargé in Peking. Contemporaneously the French were setting out on their self-chosen mission to 'regenerate' the Mexicans, and the miscarriage of this adventure, supplemented by the emergence of Germany as the leading contender for the hegemony of Europe, put France on the inactive list in Chinese affairs.

The American Protestant crusade got off to a late start in China, but when it did so in the later 1880s it lacked nothing in vigour. The eighty missionaries present in the country in 1859 increased to 1037 forty years later, most of the arrivals coming after 1880. Sectarian in nature and fundamentalist in its beliefs, the movement stemmed from the vociferous revivalist agitation in the United States. Thus the American Home Missionary Society set out first to Protestantize the United States and then to do the same for the rest of the world. Josiah Strong, a peripatetic Congregational minister who headed this society, was certain that 'the progress of Christ's kingdom in the world' was in American hands. As 'the representative of the largest liberty, the purest Christianity, the highest civilization', the United States was destined for world empire. 'This powerful race,' he asserted, 'will move down upon Mexico, down upon Central and South America, out upon the islands of the sea, over upon Africa and beyond.'[5] Strong's book, *Our Country*, which sold more than 167,000 copies, made an excellent text for the blooming American imperialism heading in the direction of China and the attack on Spain in the Philippines in 1898.

Religious enthusiasts found other leaders in the Reverend Dwight L. Moody and John R. Mott, the latter of whom also headed the YMCA, and the Student Volunteers for Foreign Missions organized Bible study groups in the many denominational colleges scattered throughout the country. A band of young missionaries from Oberlin College in northern Ohio founded an 'Oberlin in China' as early as 1881, and the scores of small private colleges in the Middle West turned into excellent recruiting grounds for workers to answer the call from China. Their slogan was 'The Evangelization of the world in this Generation', and, as Sherwood Eddy of the Yale Union Theological Seminary put it, China was on their minds: 'When I would box every afternoon . . . and when we would run our daily mile in the gym . . . we would say, "This will carry us another mile in China." ' One of Eddy's fellow-workers was Henry

Luce, who was years later to come into control of the powerful magazine empire of *Time* Inc.

Missionaries with long years of experience in China kept their minds closed to anything beyond gospel teaching. 'The heathen are heathen,' declared the Rev. J. E. Walker, 'prone toward covetousness, lust and deceit. They habitually practise what they know to be wrong.' And on a higher plane, but voicing essentially the same opinion, Professor Henry Van Dyke of Princeton wrote, 'Missions are an absolute necessity, not only for the conversion of the heathen, but also, and much more, for the preservation of the Church. Christianity is a religion that will not keep.'[6]

A few of the missionaries realized the futility of trying to make the Chinese understand the symbolic words and phrases that were part of the heritage of ancient Judaea, for example: prophets, shepherds, wine presses, the serpent (equivalent to the dragon in China, where it was the symbol of intelligence and power), the blood of Christ, the body of Christ, and so on. Eventually the missionaries put less stress on 'sin', which they could not make intelligible to the Chinese, and more on social projects such as hospitals, dispensaries and Christian colleges. But they were also purveyors of such typically American ideas as 'free enterprise', 'private property', 'progress', and 'republicanism' or its later euphemism 'democracy', which were likewise alien to Chinese culture.

American activities in China during the 1890s met with much the same reception as French Catholics had been accorded during the 1860s. A riot in Nanking in 1891 led to the destruction of a Methodist school, followed by the circulation of another scurrilous Chinese book, *Death to the Devil's Religion*. A more serious riot broke out in Szechuan province in 1895, and the missionaries were sure that the governor, Liu Ping-chang, was culpable. Similar incidents occurred in Fukien province, and the American government entered the scene with demands upon the *tsungli yamen* for the degradation and punishment of the provincial officials. Minister Charles Denby's advice in 1895, that some Chinese town be singled out for destruction by way of reprisal, has a distinctly modern ring; and, though the advice was not taken, the State Department in Washington determined on 'an impressive demonstration which can leave no doubt in the mind of the Chinese Government or the people of the interior that the United States Government is an effective factor in securing due rights for American residents in China'.

The ultimate in this strong-arm policy was laid down by William

W. Rockhill in 1896. Rockhill's name is important because of his subsequent connection with the allegedly altruistic policy of 'the open door'. As third Assistant Secretary of State in 1896, Rockhill originated a demand that China recognize the rights of American private property and agree in advance to punish any persons involved in any anti-missionary incident. The provincial governor was to be included, 'although his only fault may be ignorance'. [7]

To these and to similar demands from Britain and France the *tsungli yamen* yielded, but not until after the German government had passed the limit in taking advantage of these anti-missionary outbreaks. In November 1897 German gunboats entered Kiaochow Bay on the south shore of Shantung province, seizing the harbour and the adjacent shore on a ninety-nine-year lease and imposing the right to exploit and develop the resources of the whole province. Two German missionaries had been killed in the interior, and this was the price exacted. To the American missionaries it was no more than just retribution. German methods would succeed in bringing the Chinese to heel, and the German government, in the words of Henry Porter, who was stationed in Shantung, 'deserves the admiration of all rightminded men, the world over'.[8] But the missionaries were wrong. A wave of violence swept over China in hatred of the foreigner and his religion, and behind this came the much greater wave of 1900 – the Boxer uprising.

Xenophobia in China had its counterpart in California, where Chinese by the thousands joined in the gold rush that started in 1849. Forty thousand, or one-sixth of this new state's population, were there five years later, and fears arose that California could develop into 'a second edition of China'.[9] Caucasians, it was assumed, were 'intellectually superior' to 'Mongolians', but sheer weight of numbers would tell in favour of the Chinese. The 'dignity of labour' was at stake, for to work side by side with 'the almond-eyed tawny-skinned Asiatic' was degrading to the 'Anglo-Saxon'. Racial amalgamation could never take place, but the frugality and industry of the Chinese, who sent their savings home to China, were the greater cause for alarm to white working-men. 'Labour seems natural to them, they are never idle,' remarked one of the fairly moderate newspapers editorially. But it was generally agreed that the state legislature should enact drastic measures – discriminatory tax laws, prohibitive fees for mining licences, deportation and exclusion.

Violence broke out first in the mining towns of the foothill and mountain counties, the white miners infuriated at the Chinese staking

claims and taking out gold. Outrages were so general by 1857 that the San Francisco newspapers, unsympathetic to the attacks, were raising the question whether exclusion was not the best remedy. Angry white miners, not necessarily citizens, descended on the Chinese in force, driving them away from their diggings, tearing up their sluice boxes, scattering their tools and goods, and beating up any on whom they could lay hands. In later years, after the gold fever had subsided, animosity flared up against them in the small market towns of the valley where the local tradesmen felt that the Chinese, who voluntarily remained apart from the community, were adding nothing to the economy of the town. They were, as one editor put it, like 'the caterpillar on the leaf that first defiles and then devours'. In San Francisco the followers of the Irish boss, Denis Kearny, found numerous ways to make life miserable for the Chinese, bullying them in the streets and cutting off the queue which every Chinese man wore down his back.

Many of these unfortunates were coolies brought in from Hong-kong and Canton on contract and exploited by such capitalists as Leland Stanford and Charles Crocker in doing the hard work on the railroad being built across the High Sierra. The railroad having been completed in 1869, this redundant labour force herded into the

19 Chinatown, San Francisco. From the *Illustrated London News*, 1875.

20 Anti-Chinese feeling in California satirized by the English journalist George Sala, 1888.

Chinatowns of San Francisco and the smaller cities, where it made easy victims for dissatisfied white labourers and local demagogues. The worst incident occurred in Los Angeles, in 1890 a town of six thousand, where a mob of one thousand burned the Chinese section to the ground and killed twenty-five of its inhabitants.

Anti-Chinese clubs were common in the rural communities, and in 1886 an 'anti-Chinese Non-Partisan Association' was organized in Sacramento with the intent of making its influence felt throughout the state. Chinese labour and Chinese-produced goods, the association declared, should be boycotted. Moreover, it was 'the duty of all the people to aid in the good work of ridding the State of the Chinese now here, and of preventing any more Chinese from coming'. Occasionally gangs of men forcibly expelled the local Chinese from their towns.

Labour troubles in the orange orchards of Southern California and in the grape vineyards and hop ranches farther to the north, especially virulent in years of depression like 1893, were threatening enough to induce employers to replace Chinese labour with more highly paid whites. A similar pattern of racial behaviour evolved in Australia over the same period of time, leading eventually to the 'White Australia' policy of that commonwealth.

West coast efforts to get rid of the Chinese, or at least to halt further immigration, having come to naught, California congressmen took up the cause in Washington. Burlingame's treaty stared them in the face, as did certain constitutional and statutory guarantees which thwarted the state legislature. The practical motivation behind the Burlingame treaty still remains a puzzle, particularly since anti-Chinese feeling had surfaced many times in California before 1868 when the treaty was signed. Fears of what was to be familiarized as the 'yellow peril' – the spectre of China with its four hundred millions inundating the white nations – penetrated the American national psyche to the point where, by 1882, it was possible to enact a measure prohibiting immigration from the Orient for a period of ten years, at the end of which time a congressman from San Francisco successfully put through a strict measure which he promised would protect American labour from 'the imported paupers of the Old World'. The American government then persuaded an obliging but helpless Chinese government, which had had enough spirit to protest against the legislation, to agree to a new treaty which 'absolutely prohibited' further immigration from China. This remained the fixed rule for the next half-century. But when in 1905 Japan emerged from its triumph over Russia, the 'yellow peril' took on a new meaning. Like the Chinese, Japanese immigrants aroused fear and jealousy on the West coast and a wave of anti-Japanese legislation, which we shall describe later, soon rose.

21 'Le Partage de l'Amérique'. Cartoon by Albert Robida (Paris, 1883) satirizing the American fear of the 'Yellow Peril'.

5 American imperialism in the Orient and its frustrations

'I am afraid we are tinkering with a cracked kettle.' The words were Sir Robert Hart's and they were spoken to William Martin, the distinguished American missionary who had made himself useful in Peking, not in religious activity so much as in trying to inculcate the principles of international law in the minds of the officials of the *tsungli yamen* and of other bureaux close to the central government. Both men had staked their careers on helping to preserve the independence and integrity of China. This meant, as it were, teaching the Chinese mandarins to adopt the Western system of independent sovereign states. For thirty years Hart had been confidential adviser to the *yamen*, helping it meet every crisis with foreign powers, including a short war with France in 1884-85 and friction with Britain over the latter's annexation of Burma.

Martin had spent three-quarters of his life in China, publishing in 1896 a book which he called *A Cycle of Cathay*, the cycle being the years between China's first disaster at the hands of Britain in 1840 and its most recent at the hands of Japan in 1894-95. 'It is not China that is falling to pieces,' remarked Hart as he witnessed the sequel to Japan's triumph. 'It is the Powers that are pulling her to pieces. . . . I begin to realize how wild and wicked men can be when ruin is impending and hope of betterment gone. [The Powers] are all pegging away in one direction or another, and it all tends to loosen and disintegrate. . . . Poor China; even yet they'll not wake up to the necessity for real reform. They can be hammered and hectored into giving up anything, but no advice – no warning – will rouse them to strengthening their backbone or sharpening their claws.'[1]

The unsympathetic Charles Denby, American minister to China since 1885, decided that the country was on the verge of chaos, and that the fault lay in 'the overweening conceit' of the governing classes: 'Proud, haughty, bound up in ceremonial, absolutely ignorant of foreign affairs, the rulers of China are the least intelligent of her respectable people.' Denby was a lawyer from the American Middle West whose models of conduct were businessmen. Chinese merchants and bankers made 'a splendid contrast' to the mandarins – their word was as good as their bond. Of Chinese customs and culture he made it clear that he wanted to know nothing. Railways were the cure for China's ills, and only Western, particularly American, capital and skill could do the job. Americans built the best railroads, and Denby had not been long in the country when he undertook to apply his convictions: he tried (unsuccessfully) for a concession for his business acquaintance, General James Wilson of the New England Railroad Company, that would bring American capital into the country and employ American engineers and materials. His reflections on teaching English to the Chinese speak volumes: 'The educated Chinaman, who speaks English, becomes a new man; he commences to think.' In Richard Olney, a corporation lawyer who became Secretary of State in 1895, Denby found a kindred spirit. And in their own way the foreign missionaries, both English and American, held to the same attitude. 'China is a huge anachronism,' declared a British Protestant publication. 'The best thing Europe and America can do for China at the present crisis is to give it the gospel of Jesus Christ more freely.' 2

Denby's beliefs and ambitions were already gospel to British business interests in China, notably to the Shanghai Chamber of Commerce which, aware that the Tientsin treaties had not really opened up the interior, had in 1869 initiated a move to induce the British government to take a hand. But the latter, having established a diplomatic mission at Peking and consulates at Shanghai and other treaty ports, had decided on a policy of non-intervention. Grievances of British subjects were to be handled by the consuls and the ambassador in negotiation with the *tsungli yamen*, just as they would be in any other country.

When the French by war forced the Chinese to retire from Indochina in favour of France, they gave the alarm to British interests both at home and in China: China's two provinces in the south-west, Yunnan and Szechuan, were in the path of a possible further French advance. Although still sealed to the outside world, these provinces were thought to offer glittering opportunities for the future. Old China hands at the treaty ports were used to seeing all of China from the Yangtze valley south as a natural monopoly reserved for them. In Archibald R. Colquhoun, special correspondent for *The Times* and Denby's contemporary in China, British interests found an ardent supporter. Colquhoun attracted the attention of various chambers of commerce in Britain, and the merchants grew importunate in their demands on the British government to lend them a hand. The government, however, kept to its negative position until 1895, when the merchants set up the China Association with the announced purpose of marking off spheres of interest. A Russian move into

向壊無敵
平壌陥落

22 The Sino-Japanese War in Korea, 1895. Japanese woodblock print.

Manchuria at this time added to the alarm. The China Association took the view that the Continental powers, if left unchecked, would snip off parts of China, and little by little the British would lose their leading position. To keep ahead of the game they must have government help.

The first direct assault on China came from Japan in 1894, the end result of a running dispute over Korea, traditionally one of the tributary states of the Middle Kingdom. At this point a note on the importance of semantics is in order. It will be remembered that tribute bearers to the court of Peking submitted to a ritual, including the kotow, which signified their subordinate status as barbarians, but that in other respects they were left to their own devices, independent *de facto*. The nearest Western equivalent to this ancient Chinese conception of cultural superiority is the doctrine of a sphere of

67

influence (or of interest) whereby the societies (or nations) within the sphere of a given power are targets for cultural and economic penetration by that power. The United States, in its effort to be 'different', had blanketed the 'Western hemisphere' with its Monroe Doctrine, which at this very time was on the threshold of becoming an open declaration of hemispheric hegemony.

Japan, whose political system, it has been suggested, bore an affinity to Western ideas of national sovereignty and independence, in 1876 prised open Korea, the 'Land of Morning Calm', on the basis of its 'independence', a legalistic status that suited the interests of the Western treaty powers, especially of the United States. In Japanese books, however, Korean 'independence' meant a sphere of influence for Japan, an objective made clear by the outbreak of war with China in 1894. Encouraged by Japanese success since the Meiji restoration in emulating Western ideas of progress, a small group of Americans centring on General Wilson, Charles Denby and a few others, intrigued to induce the Japanese government to pursue the war into Peking itself overthrowing the Ch'ing dynasty and putting Li Hung-chang, the one Chinese official whom they respected, in power over North China. China, or at least that portion of it ruled by Li Hung-chang, would then be available for 'development'. But these men did not understand the obstacles in their path: Li's unwillingness to abandon the concept of China as symbolized by the dynasty and to become, in effect, a catspaw for selfish foreign interests; and Japan's unreadiness to prosecute the war to so decisive a conclusion. The Japanese obtained from China an admission of the 'independence' of Korea; and they hoped, but in vain, to keep the Liaotung peninsula for themselves as a springboard for later adventures in Manchuria and North China. Sir Robert Hart grasped the point. 'Japanese ambition is growing,' he declared, 'and they now talk of *ruling* China, and refusing all foreign intervention.'[3]

According to John W. Foster, a former American Secretary of State who was called to Peking to accompany Li as an adviser to the peace conference, the more moderate members of the Japanese delegation realized that Russia could effectively exercise a veto over the retention of Liaotung, but the military party insisted upon keeping the peninsula as the spoils of war. Not only did the Russians intervene – Li Hung-chang expected them to – but they brought both France and Germany to their support. The war ended in 1895 with China demoralized – even Hart had lost hope – and with Japan victorious, but outraged and frustrated by Russia's gratuitous interference.

Years before this war Korea had become the 'happy hunting-ground of the concessionists', and in the forefront of these eager speculators was the American medical missionary, Horace N. Allen. As in China, missionaries were not welcome in Korea, although Japan tended to favour them as a civilizing influence. Practitioners of medicine had the advantage, and within a year after his arrival in Seoul in 1884 Allen performed the small miracle of making himself the king's favourite. As such he lost no time in seeking privileges for other missionaries and for American businessmen. His most remarkable achievement was a gold-mining concession north of the thirty-eighth parallel, incorporated after more than five years of effort as the Oriental Consolidated Mining Company which, with the exception of a few years of losses, paid handsome dividends between 1895 and 1939, the year of its demise. Being the most influential foreigner in the country, Allen pursued his ambition to make Korea an American protectorate at least in disguise; but in this respect the Japanese allowed him no elbow room.

Meanwhile concession hunting started in earnest in China, fully justifying Sir Robert Hart's pessimism. Years earlier a German geographer had pointed to the advantages of Kiaochow Bay on the south coast of Shantung, and in 1896 Admiral von Tirpitz decided that this was the place for a German naval base. A Chinese mob attack on German missionaries was expected to furnish the necessary incident, and so it turned out, as we have seen, in November 1897. The Germans set to work on their new port of Tsingtao, and their provocative behaviour in surveying for mining and railway rights in the interior of the province poured fuel on the fires of xenophobia already burning fiercely.

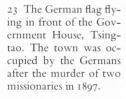

23 The German flag flying in front of the Government House, Tsingtao. The town was occupied by the Germans after the murder of two missionaries in 1897.

This German forwardness in detaching Shantung from China forced a change in Russian plans as outlined by Count Witte, the Minister of the Interior and builder of the Trans-Siberian Railway. Witte conceived of a gradual advance through Manchuria and on to Peking, where Russia could take its time in making itself the overlord of China. But with Germany as a partner, Russia decided to limit its sphere to Manchuria and to a lease of the Liaotung peninsula, which it had denied to Japan. The peninsula meant a naval base at Port Arthur and a seaport town on Talienwan. These moves, consummated in the spring of 1898, stirred the British government to make its first forward step in China – a lease of Weihaiwei on the north coast of Shantung, which turned out to be the opening gesture towards the alliance with Japan in 1902.

Naturally the British China Association looked with dismay upon the encroachments of the other powers. The French contributed their share by extorting a concession at Kwangchowwan in Kwangtung province. Railways built under the auspices of other powers and penetrating into the heart of the Yangtze valley threatened to deprive British commerce of its advantages derived from the river traffic. Thus a north-south line from Tientsin to Nanking, a line projected by the American China Development Company for a connection between Hankow and Canton, and a French-built line from Indochina

into one of the interior provinces, were all dangerous possibilities to the Shanghai Chamber of Commerce. The association now wanted the Yangtze valley set aside as a special British sphere and a recognition of an 'open door' to trade throughout all parts of China. The expression 'open door' was now common currency, made so by the international rivalries sketched in the foregoing paragraphs. Spokesmen for the association alluded to Cecil Rhodes of Southern Africa as the kind of a leader they wanted for British interests in China. Without being explicit, they favoured an 'effective occupation' of the Yangtze valley and a government guarantee of bank loans for capital developments. To these proposals Lord Salisbury, speaking for the government, gave a flat negative on 9 June 1899. The date is important because it was three months before the so-called 'open door notes' of John Hay. Said Salisbury, 'We cannot make the Yangtze Valley a province like Shantung or Manchuria, first, because it is infinitely larger, and secondly, we are not prepared to undertake the immense responsibility of governing what is practically a third of China.'

The concluding view taken by Nathan Pelcovits, whose book *Old China Hands and the Foreign Office* establishes the difference between the pressures exerted by the private mercantile interests and the policy of the government, will further underscore the meaning of

24, 25 Popular national reactions to the German and British presence in China during the late nineteenth century. The German postcard, left, dated 1899, expresses national pride in the bestowal of German citizenship on the Chinese of Tsingtao, declared a free port by the Germans in that year. The advertisement for Brooke's Tea, right, alludes to Britain's satisfaction at acquiring a lease of Weihaiwei in 1898.

GOOD FOR CHINA! "WEI-HAI-WEI!!!"

the Salisbury statement. Refusal to heed these pressures, says Pelcovits, 'solves the historical riddle of why China never became another India'.[4]

Among the concession hunters none could have been busier than the business-minded missionary, Horace N. Allen, who operated a sort of one-man show in Korea. Having ingratiated himself at court, Allen headed a Korean diplomatic mission to Washington, DC, stressing Korean 'independence' from China; and upon his return he started up the ladder in the American legation, soon to occupy the top post. Through it he obtained concessions for himself and his friends – a gold mine, a railway, a trolley line and an electric lighting company in Seoul. But his indirect political control died in 1905, when Japan took over the country and kept it for forty years, at the end of which time Korea began a new cycle, its southern half emerging as a foster-child of the United States.

In Peking Charles Denby was no less diligent than Allen, though rival actors crowded him on the Chinese stage. Denby, John W. Foster, whose friendship with Li Hung-chang was very convenient, and General James Wilson hoped to win a franchise for a trunk line running from Peking to Canton, although they encountered competition from another group of American capitalists headed by Senator Calvin Brice, a corporation lawyer from Ohio. Secretary of State Olney signalled Denby in 1895 to go ahead. It was these Americans who chiefly imperilled the British monopoly over the Yangtze valley.

Wilson negotiated to set up a syndicate that would get the ear of Li Hung-chang in Peking and of the tsar in St Petersburg. An alliance with the Trans-Siberian Railway would create an omnipotent transportation system; and if the Russians would admit the Americans to a share in the Trans-Siberian, the latter could make a bid for the economic domination of all Asia. But they learned first-hand of the Russian determination to keep foreigners away from the Trans-Siberian and its Manchurian subsidiaries, and a Franco-Belgian syndicate beat them to it in offering terms for a franchise covering a line from Peking to Hankow. Neither of the American groups possessed the assets to see them through on even the smaller of these projects, and moral encouragement was the most they could get out of the government in Washington. Nevertheless, the second group, which called itself the American China Development Company, went ahead in 1898 with a speculation on a franchise it won for a line from Hankow to Canton; but this too fell apart in a few years for the same

Locomotives for Export

A Baldwin Locomotive for Service in China

26 An advertisement (1919) for the Baldwin Locomotive Works, an American company with agents in Shanghai and Tokyo.

reason – the unreadiness of New York capitalists to put money into a country so near a state of collapse as China.

China, however, was still the lure – for business as for religion. The sudden outburst of missionary zeal in the 1890s was matched by the impatience of businessmen to cash in on 'the greatest of world markets'. 'In China,' exclaimed a bankers' magazine in 1898, 'there are four hundred millions of people, more than five times as many as exist in the United States. The wants of four hundred millions are increasing every year. What a market!'[5] American merchants and manufacturers thought in the same frame of reference as the old China hands of the treaty ports. Clichés like 'China's awakening' and the 'markets of Cathay' caught the American fancy, especially with the visit of Li Hung-chang himself in 1896.

John W. Foster got Li to tour the United States on his return trip from Moscow, where the Russians had paid him honours. Secretary Olney rode with him in an open carriage down Fifth Avenue. Olney needed no convincing of the need for 'more markets and larger markets for the consumption of the products of industry'. The panic of 1893, which had brought down the great house of Baring overseas and dried up the domestic markets for manufactured goods in America as well as in Britain, fired the spirit of competition for foreign markets. The surplus could not be sold at home or in Europe, where industry had likewise got ahead of itself. South America was one area which had scarcely been tapped, but China was a better. It was a cry to 'export or die', as Hitler was to put it to the Germans some forty years after. Big business, like the Baldwin Locomotive Works, Bethlehem Iron and the Cramp Shipbuilding Company courted Li for contracts; and smaller concerns joined in the National Association of Manufacturers. These too dreamed of the new day in the East: 'We must make our plans to secure our full share of the great trade which is coming out of the new industrial era in the Orient.'[6] A canal dug across Central America – Nicaragua most probably, but perhaps Panama – was by this time a practical possibility, and it would help to restore the United States to primacy in the trade of Asia. Taking as its model the British China Association, the American Asiatic Association established itself in New York in 1899 and opened branches in Shanghai and Japan. Captains of industry, large corporations, even a government official or two like William Woodville Rockhill and the now retired Charles Denby, were among its 242 members concerned with enlisting government support.

Meanwhile the United States was fast pushing on with its forward movement across the Pacific. Hawaii, the 'half-way house to the great markets of the East', was annexed in June 1898. It was the crossroads which insured strategic control of the North Pacific. The missionaries, whose activities in the islands reached back almost a century, were in full agreement. Hawaii was 'a great lighthouse and a base of operations for the enterprise of universal evangelization'.[7] Manila, conceived of as an 'American Hongkong', was already in American hands. Eyes were upon it at least as early as September 1897, and it was the first object of attack in the following April.

27 On 7 July 1898 President McKinley signed the Resolution annexing Hawaii to the United States. Cartoon in *Punch*, 1898.

Cuba furnished the pretext – the necessary war fever had been worked up on behalf of Cuban freedom-fighters against Spain. But Cuba too commanded high strategic value: the island was a 'blockhouse' for the projected inter-oceanic canal, the eastern end of the 'life-line' of the China trade. The United States had had designs on it since the days of Thomas Jefferson.

The Philippines were the 'pickets of the Pacific, standing guard at the entrances to trade with the millions of China and Korea, French Indo-China, the Malay Peninsula, and the islands of Indonesia'.[8] The naval attack on the Spanish squadron in Manila Bay – ordered on 25 February 1898 and executed by the American fleet based at Hongkong as soon as hostilities broke out in April – was followed by the speedy dispatch of an expeditionary force from San Francisco to take possession of the island archipelago. Orders to assemble this expedition were actually issued three days *before* intelligence had reached Washington of the outcome of the naval engagement. The subsequent outbreak of a Filipino war of independence proved embarrassing and troublesome to put down, but knowledge that Germany meant to exploit the insurrection sealed American determination not to let any of the islands escape. The Germans, not satisfied with Kiaochow, wanted a 'Hongkong' for themselves in South China waters, but the United States forestalled them. Meanwhile, in June-July 1898 it filled in the lifeline between Hawaii and the Philippines with two intermediate points, Guam which it needed as a coaling station and Wake Island as a cable landing.

Placed thus in position for a new drive on the China market, American foreign service officers conceived of a leasehold in China itself. Edwin R. Conger, Denby's successor at Peking, proposed a foothold in Chihli, the metropolitan province; the new consul at Amoy, aware of its spacious harbour, wanted a concession there. Geographically Amoy was in direct line with Manila, connected by regular steamship service, and among the old treaty ports it ranked high. The consul feared Japan would get it, and he preferred it to Hongkong. It 'is the one port in China we must preserve,' he urged, 'if we are to make of our new possessions in the Orient what is now anticipated.' Alternatives were Chefoo on the north side of Shantung, some site on the Chekiang coast or, best of all from the standpoint of the navy, the Chusan islands off the mouth of the Yangtze. The *Forum* magazine published an article on the subject in February 1899, written by a ranking officer in the Navy Department. 'With the recent concessions made by China in the way of granting territory to

75

other first-class nations,' he observed, 'it would appear that the United States might, with becoming modesty, ask for one of these islands.'[9] But instead John Hay secretly sounded out Japan regarding its reaction to a possible lease of Samsah Bay in the vicinity of Amoy. From Japan, as might be expected, came a negative response – Formosa was just opposite and was in Japanese hands – and for this and perhaps other reasons Hay decided not to press the issue.

These cautious moves were so many straws in the wind, easily blown away. But the United States was in the curious position in 1899 of seeing its lifeline to China completed but not capable of being put to the use expected of it. Manila was not enough; Mr Conger pointed that out. Some workable alternative had to be discovered. The initiative came from Alfred E. Hippisley, a native of Bristol, England, and for thirty-odd years a career man in the Inspectorate of Maritime Customs under Sir Robert Hart. Like Hart, Hippisley understood Chinese and had benefited from cultural assimilation by China far more than most Europeans. He realized that conditions in China had so changed as to render the treaty ports and the 'open door' system, as exemplified by the customs service, at least partially obsolete; and he especially feared Russian encroachment from Manchuria. But when, in August 1899, the tsar decreed Dalny, the new town on the Liaotung peninsula, a free port, Hippisley felt encouraged. He got the ear of John Hay through their mutual friend Rockhill.

Rockhill too had an intimate acquaintance with China: five years as secretary to the legation in Peking, a knowledge of the language, an adventurous journey into the heart of Tibet. But he held to an unbending belief that China must be taught to accept the responsibilities and obligations which were standard among Western nations. Like the businessmen and the missionaries, he rejoiced in the Japanese victory of 1895: it was a good object-lesson to the Chinese, a demonstration of 'progress'. The Chinese must learn how to protect foreigners, and the central government must pay when trouble occurred. Rockhill was unwilling to make any allowance for the decentralized nature of the Chinese socio-political structure; and he seemed to think that, in spite of the corruption in the Ch'ing régime, the mandarins would reform if punished enough.

The open door was already a catch phrase which had changed meaning several times. The British China Association exploited it as a response to the sphere of influence system, and the American Asiatic Association adopted it with enthusiasm in 1899. As outlined

28 American diplomacy 'opens the door' to trade with the delighted Chinese, while Britain and Russia watch. Cartoon in *Life*, 1900.

by Lord Charles Beresford, who spoke for the British Chambers of Commerce, it involved a grandiose scheme for a British-American-German-Japanese alliance which would force reforms upon China, reorganize the army under foreign advisers, and so make a reality of the country's 'independence and integrity'. The Asiatic Association primed Hay on its programme, linked 'integrity' with commercial development, and made the issue a moral question of United States leadership: 'The US undoubtedly stands today as the strongest influence for the integrity of the Chinese empire.'

Beresford was a great success in the United States, though Rockhill regarded him as 'a bag of wind'. Between his book, *The Break-up of China*, and his many speeches, he promoted the open door as a crusade for China's benefit: 'We have a big, honest idea of what should be done with trade and commerce, and we have, even better than that, a grand, chivalrous, noble sentiment in regard to what should be done with weaker nations.'[10]

Hippisley's proposal, made privately through correspondence, was more conservative. It was simply that the United States make public

29 Uncle Sam, asserting the straightforward nature of his motives in wishing to trade with the Chinese, holds back the European countries which long to join him ('A Fair Field and no Favor', *Harper's Weekly*, 1899).

its position that its treaty rights in China were to be respected. Railway building, the development of mines and other capital investments might be of separate national origin; but differential tariffs on merchandise, discriminatory harbour dues in the leased ports and freight rates were not to be tolerated. In other words, Hippisley proposed to rescue the treaty system as conducted by the customs service. To this Rockhill added the ideas of 'reform' and 'integrity', which were already favourites of his. It was Rockhill who drafted Hay's 'open door notes' of 5 September 1899, which became an American national legend. The notes did not attempt the impossible: they contained no challenge to the 'sphere of interest' or the leased territory concept. They only asked each power to respect the treaty system.

Applause from the newspaper and magazine press greeted the notes. China's independence was assured. Furthermore, the United States now 'has something to say as to the future of Asia, and, if need comes, it will have something to do'. Rockhill himself cultivated the notion in an article for *Forum* in May 1900. America was different from the predatory European powers. Chinese independence was a fact because America, by its note-writing, had made it so. It is strange that Rockhill should have so lost himself in self-praise: in private

78

communications to John Hay he had emphatically stated that the spheres of influence were facts. Russia in particular had too good a hold on Manchuria, and in responding to Hay it side-stepped any commitment that it would relinquish the advantages of its railway network and its possession of the one good port of entry.

There was another catch to the verbal miracle performed by Hay and Rockhill. The Americans were lost in admiration for what they had done for China. Discounting the Boxer uprising, which broke out within three months after Hay's notes, they assumed that there would be an almost automatic administrative reform in that country. The Chinese, now that the United States had made it possible for them, would create an efficient central government whose authority would be respected in all the provinces. But this was a concept alien to the Chinese mind, impossible of application even if there had been no threat of internal rebellion. So the foreign powers, including the United States, fell back again on the practice of imposing heavy penalties for damage done to foreign life and property.

The outrages perpetrated by the Germans in Shantung and by the Russians in Manchuria stirred the populace to fury. To stand aside while their villages were burned in retaliation for some incidental attack on a Christian was too much. Chinese Christians were a sort of privileged class, protected by the missionaries and by the guns behind the missionaries. When trouble occurred, according to the governor of Shantung province, 'the local officials, afraid of incurring foreign hostility, usually settle the cases in favour of the Christians'. Secret societies, such as the Big Sword with a long background of ritualistic practices and anti-foreign activities, came out into the open under the general name of Boxers, so-called because of a boxing ritual they had developed. Floods and famines brought on by another flood of the Yellow river and other natural disasters meant untold misery for the masses of Chihli and Shantung provinces.

Organized violence broke out in Chihli in October 1898, spreading north-westward to Tientsin and on to Peking, which the insurgents took over in June 1900. Railroads and telegraph lines, symbols of foreign oppression, were special objects of attack. 'Uphold the Ch'ing, exterminate the foreigners.' This was the war-cry of the Boxers, with whom a section of the imperial court, led by the Empress Dowager, secretly collaborated. Yüan Shih-k'ai, the new governor of Shantung who had gained his laurels as Chinese resident in Korea, received orders not to interfere with the Boxers. A hastily organized international expedition under the British Admiral

30 An imaginary scene depicted in a Chinese woodcut, *c.* 1900. Foreign prisoners are brought before General Tung, before their trial and execution.

Seymour set out from Tientsin for the relief of the legations in Peking, but it was thrown back and the railway cut, a victory which encouraged the Boxers and left the legations isolated and protected only by a force of approximately five hundred regular guards and volunteers.

A siege of the legations followed, continuing through part of the summer of 1900, the rest of Peking being given over to rioting and plunder while the imperial court fled inland. In July the murder of Baron von Kettler, the German minister who had made himself particularly obnoxious to the Chinese, dramatized the scene to the outside world and spurred the assemblage of an international relief expedition (in which the United States, drawing upon troops from the Philippines, participated). But while annihilation was the announced object of the siege, its actual conduct showed division of opinion and uncertainty among the Chinese. Of those at the top an intelligent minority were cognizant of the vengeance the Western powers would wreak in the event of a general massacre. Sir Robert Hart remarked on how the soldiery kept 'playing with us as cats do with mice', on 'the curiously half-hearted character' of the siege

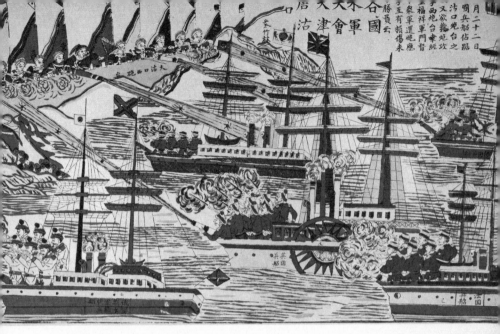

31 Foreign ships bombarding the Yuka ports after the outbreak of the Boxer rebellion in 1900. Chinese woodcut.

which 'not only gave us the chance to live through it, but also gave any relief forces time to come and extricate us, and thus avert the national calamity which the Palace in its pride and conceit ignored.' A sensational episode at the time, the siege when reduced to its proper proportions appears 'as a small incident in the vast history of China'.[11]

The allied success in reaching Peking on 14 August 1900 broke up the siege and terminated the Boxer uprising. The provinces of South China had remained relatively unaffected, and the good faith shown by the viceroys of these provinces had deceived men like Rockhill into thinking that China could be reformed. But Rockhill was as adamant as ever that China must meet all of its foreign obligations, including fresh indemnities to be imposed for the losses incurred during the uprising. Rockhill was appointed American representative in negotiating the settlement with Li Hung-chang, whom the imperial court recalled from his retirement in Canton; and in terms of the amounts China was to pay the several powers, Rockhill was more moderate than his European colleagues. He was also uninfluenced by the cries for vengeance which arose from the missionaries. A policy

BELIEVE ON THE LORD JESUS CHRIST AND THOU SHALT BE SAVED.

LET HIM THAT HEARETH SAY, COME!

32 An illustration from *The Pictorial Missionary News* (London, 1871).

statement issued by four hundred American and British missionaries demanded severe punishment of all high Chinese officials implicated in the uprising, heavy damages and replacement costs for missionary property destroyed, and foreign supervision of the imperial government. Individual missionaries, travelling in groups, set out to impose their own terms on Chinese villagers: special cemeteries for martyred Christians, money for building Christian chapels, assessments one-third in excess of the value of mission property destroyed. Two American missionaries in particular were very enterprising in this respect: the Reverend William Ament and the Reverend E. G. Tewkesbury, who like the Reverend Henry Porter preferred 'the mailed fist of the Germans' to what they regarded as American softness. Missionary fanaticism invited criticism in the American press, including one of Mark Twain's wittiest satires addressed 'To the Person Sitting in Darkness'. Shall we, Mark Twain wanted to know, 'go on conferring our Civilization upon the peoples that sit in darkness, or shall we give those poor things a rest?'

American attention was now more than ever riveted upon China, and so we must stop and take account of the several schools of thought on the subject that matured around the turn of the century. Far from feeling abashed at the hostile demonstrations against them, the missionaries redoubled their efforts to 'bring Christ' to the Chinese. And, *mirabile dictu*, they made considerable headway, so much so as to mislead prominent missionaries like Bishop Bashford of the Methodist Church and Sherwood Eddy and John R. Mott from Yale into thinking that China really was on the high road to Christianity and Western education. Revivalist meetings remained in the forefront of missionary activities, but Christian schools and colleges, some of them dating back to Bible schools of the mid-nineteenth century, made their mark. Missionaries also educated the church-going public in America on the troubles of China, emphasizing its backwardness and idolatry. The inferior status of women and the cruel practice of binding the feet of little girls gave point to these denigrations. Arthur H. Smith, one of the most widely read of the missionary writers, went beyond these criticisms by insisting that deceitfulness was a peculiarly Chinese characteristic. 'What the Chinese lack,' he wrote, 'is not intellectual ability. It is not patience, practicality, nor cheerfulness, for in all these qualities they greatly excel. What they do lack is Character and Conscience.'[12]

Both by word and by deed the missionaries conveyed the impression that China was an inferior country which it was America's duty to 'save'. Living in compounds and retaining control of their several activities in American hands, they ignored the undercurrent of resentment flowing in the direction of the revolution that broke out in the next decade. Their religiosity also blinded them to the fact that the educated Confucian mentality did not care for Christian theology, though it did find common ground with Western pragmatism and scepticism.

Variations upon the theme of imperial America impinging upon Asia are to be found in the writings of Whitelaw Reid, editor of the *New York Tribune* and later ambassador to Britain; of Alfred Thayer Mahan, the great philosopher of sea power; of Brooks Adams of the famous Boston family, who had developed a theory of the 'Law of Civilization and Decay'; and of Charles A. Conant who, as editor of the *Banker's Magazine*, expressed the thinking of the financial community. All four used the war with Spain as their point of departure, depicting the United States on the threshold of world empire as a result of its island conquests.

Reid blended ideas of duty, interest, power, influence and trade into a concise creed. 'The shrewd Oriental,' he declared, 'no longer regards us as a second or third class power', but as 'a nation that knows its rights and dares maintain them – a nation that has come to stay, with an empire of its own in the China Sea, and a navy which . . . will be able to defend it against the world.' Its missionaries 'must be endured with patience and even protected', and its 'friendship must be sedulously cultivated.' A new field was 'opened for our reaping. Planted directly in front of the Chinese colossus, on a great territory of our own, we have the first and best chance to profit by his awakening. Commanding both sides of the Pacific . . . we command the ocean that . . . is to bear the bulk of the world's commerce in the twentieth century.'[13]

Mahan, a more cautious thinker, was reconciled to dividing the field with Germany, Britain and Japan, with whom the United States had interests in common. The 'yellow peril' was a possibility in his mind – the danger of a united China eventually pitting itself against the European family of nations to which the United States belonged. But the more immediate threat came from Russia, which had planted itself in Manchuria. It was up to the sea powers, notably Britain and America, to keep China away from the Russian embrace; and, not foreseeing the startling success that Japan, the newest of the sea powers, was soon to have in expelling Russia from South Manchuria, Mahan advocated abandoning north China and concentrating upon the Yangtze, up which warships could penetrate deep into the interior. Peking was uncomfortably close to the Russian border, and the Chinese should be induced to move their seat of government to a location within the Anglo-American sphere of influence. Mahan took it for granted that China would remain permanently weak, and he could not pay even lip service to the fiction of Chinese independence and integrity. Christianity was a civilizing influence – it had been so in Europe and it could be promoted to the same end in China – hence the missionaries should be encouraged.

Brooks Adams ignored the missionaries and fastened his attention on the economic supremacy and the transfer of power that he held was now within the grasp of the United States. His yardstick was the lead in the production of steel obtained, according to him, in March 1897; and the coming struggle for power would be over the mines of Shansi and Honan in central and eastern China. So, unlike Mahan, Adams would by no means abdicate in north China but would contend with Russia for the mastery of that country. America was the 'New Empire', the successor to Britain, but the centre of its interests was no longer the Atlantic but the Pacific, 'which it will hold like an island sea'. Manila was 'the natural focus . . . the military and commercial key to eastern Asia. Entrenched there, and backing on Europe, with force enough to prevent our competitors from closing the Chinese mainland against us by discrimination, there is no reason why the United States should not become a greater seat of wealth and power than ever was England, Rome, or Constantinople.' The whole world would be forced into paying tribute. But fear of falling short of this goal, and of the fatal consequences that would follow, occupied Adams's mind, and again China would be the testing-ground. 'The United States could hardly contemplate with equanimity the successful organization of a hostile industrial system on the shores of the Pacific, based on Chinese labour, nourished by European capital, and supplied by the inexhaustible resources of the valley of the Ho-hang-ho.'[14]

From this frenzy of fear and ambition depicting an ordeal by battle between the United States and the rest of the world over the body of China we turn to the theory of the economist, Charles A. Conant, as set forth in his book *The United States in the Orient*, published in 1900. Like the English Fabian socialist, J. A. Hobson, Conant is preoccupied with the problem of surplus capital accumulated in Western Europe and America and how to find outlets for its continued investment. Conant and Hobson agreed that a serious situation had emerged from the 'congestion of saved capital' and the international competition for investment opportunities that was certain to develop. In a powerful polemic against imperialism which he published two years later, Hobson deplored the spirit of cut-throat competition, developed a guilt thesis with respect to international bankers, but in the end had to confess that the process could not be checked. Hobson's concluding chapter carries an apocalyptic note. Imperialism, he maintained, is 'a depraved choice of national life . . . the besetting sin of all successful States, and its penalty is unalterable in the order of nature'.[15] Brooks Adams is the antithesis of Hobson. Both regard the USA as the classic land of imperialism, Adams urging it on, Hobson sparing no language in condemning it. But of the two, Adams was more of the fatalist: eventually Western society would crack. Meanwhile, however, the American empire could flourish by reason of its head start in the Pacific and the Orient.

Conant is more detached than either of these writers, but his predilections are definitely for the empire. After describing how the

supply of surplus capital has led to the creation of great banking institutions, he launches into an exposition of the United States as a world power, whose principal enemy is the Russian empire, 'the greatest organized force which confronts Western civilization'. China, which was about to be gridironed with railways, was a natural outlet for the surplus, a country where the United States could meet Russia on better than even terms. Pointing to the achievement of British capital in Egypt under the guidance of Lord Cromer, Conant was confident that wise American leadership would be forthcoming for a similar accomplishment in China. A world market open under conditions of equal opportunity 'will command the support not alone of the business community, but of all far-seeing men who desire the perpetuation of the ideals of Anglo-Saxon civilization'.[16]

None of these writers, not even Captain Mahan, gave proper credit to the role that Japan was about to play on the stage in northeast Asia. Having obtained the upper hand in Korea, the Japanese stepped forward after their share in the Boxer settlement to protest against the Russian failure to withdraw from Manchuria. By October 1900, after the danger to the foreign legations in Peking was over, Russian forces were in possession of the whole of Manchuria, including the treaty port of Newchwang; and the Chinese were told to make no concessions to foreigners in either Manchuria or Mongolia without Russian consent. Li Hung-chang let this cat out of the bag in February 1901, thereby confronting the powers, especially Japan, Britain and the United States, with the necessity of deciding on some

33, 34 The Russo-Japanese War of 1904–5. Exulting Japanese sailors watch from their torpedo boat as two Russian ships sink. Woodcut by Toshidide. Right, Japanese cartoon, showing Tsar Nicholas II playing with models of the Russian army and navy.

sort of a policy. Inside circles in St Petersburg were split on whether to accede to British and Japanese urgings to withdraw, but the war party headed by General Kuropatkin had its way. It also refused to compromise with Britain regarding other areas of friction, notably Iran; and the outcome of this attitude was the Anglo-Japanese alliance of 1902.

Symptoms of American-Russian antagonism appeared at the lowest level in the port of Newchwang, where Russian and American sailors were marooned for the winter. Their bar-room brawls brought headaches for the consular authorities. The American minister in Peking, Edwin Conger, was positive Russia meant to detach Manchuria from China and thought the United States would be the loser. Conger's point of view, expounded in September 1901, was subsequently adopted as a basis for American policy, and so is worth quoting here:

Russia will have her great Trans-Siberian railway completed in another year. Its main terminal point will be Dalny. . . . This will open up to settlement and development the only great territory, still left on the globe, so favoured with soil and climate as to promise great agricultural development and its concomitant of a strong people and resultant great trade progress. *Its contiguity to the United States* and the possibility of connecting its great railroad system by direct lines of steamers across the Pacific with our own transcontinental routes make friendly political and trade relations between the two peoples most desirable and important.[17]

But the United States did not deal with Russia direct, confident, as John Hay put it, that Japan would 'fly at the throat of Russia' if encouraged. Taking the stance that Manchuria was China's property, the American government got China to agree in October 1903 to make treaty ports out of Mukden and Antung; but, since the Russians were in actual possession, this treaty was the emptiest of diplomatic gestures, though interpreted by the Russians as a stroke against them. Meanwhile the Japanese, their direct demands on Russia having been rebuffed, did substantially what John Hay predicted. On 8 February 1904 Japanese torpedo boats attacked the Russian fleet at Port Arthur and sank it.

The sudden attack and victory delighted both the heads of the American government and the organs of public opinion. Japan was 'playing our game', 'battling on the side of civilization', and representing the 'Anglo-Saxon races'. These and similar expressions of pleasure dropped from the pens of Theodore Roosevelt, Elihu Root and others. In the future Japan should have the Yellow Sea much as the United States had the Caribbean. A balance between the belligerents should be created, leaving both of them weakened and 'a line of friction' drawn between them. But not until after Japan had taken Mukden (March 1905) and sunk a second Russian fleet (28 May 1905) were both parties ready to come to terms. As between Britain, Japan's ally, and the United States, technically a neutral, the latter was the more active. The Russian belief that Roosevelt had 'goaded' Japan into war was too strong, though there was a kernel of truth in it. 'Every time the Russians get a kick from the Japanese, they turn and swear at us', was John Hay's way of putting it. But Roosevelt did not want Japan to press on into Manchuria too far, nor did he take to the idea of it putting itself at the head of China. Indubitably there was now 'a great new force in eastern Asia' which made for possibilities of a revised version of the 'yellow peril', as the German Kaiser was ready to point out. But the Japanese themselves recognized their limitations – American and British banks aided in their war financing – and they welcomed Roosevelt's determination to act the part of peace-maker.[18]

Portsmouth, New Hampshire, was the meeting place, and Japanese and Russian terms were not basically far apart. Japan required a free hand in Korea (a stipulation to which no exception was taken), Russian army withdrawal from Manchuria, and transfer of Russian leasehold rights in the Liaotung peninsula and of the railway from Harbin to Port Arthur. But when a money indemnity large enough to meet war costs was added, Roosevelt baulked and the tsar resolved on renewing the war. This Japan could not afford to do, nor would the New York banks, notably Kuhn, Loeb and Company, allow further credits. Roosevelt expressed his viewpoint succinctly thus: 'It is Japan's interest now to close the war. She has won the control of Korea and Manchuria; she has doubled her own fleet in destroying that of Russia; she has Port Arthur, Dalny, the Manchurian railroad, she has Sakhalin.'[19]

Britain stood on the sidelines, but nevertheless while the peace conference was in session (August 1905) renewed the alliance with Japan, its terms strengthened over those of the original agreement. Korea standing in relation to Japan in American eyes as Cuba stood to the United States – a protectorate of the paramount power – there was no hesitation over formally acknowledging the fact; and a memorandum to that effect was agreed to shortly thereafter, constituting as it were an 'alliance in practice' among the three powers, as Count Katsura, the Japanese Prime Minister, accurately described it. To all appearances a perfect balance of power, which had been Roosevelt's objective, had been achieved in the region of northeast Asia.

But Manchuria, a vast undeveloped country, was too tempting a prize to be left alone for long. The Russian railway network had revealed the possibilities, and in February 1906 the Japanese foreign office attempted to guard itself against competition by securing from China, the nominal 'sovereign', a pledge not to build a 'parallel' or branch line in the neighbourhood of the South Manchurian Railway. Subsequently, in June 1907, Japan concluded a firm agreement with Russia dividing the country in two halves, the Japanese reserving the southern half as their sphere of interest which was to be open to foreign commerce but not to foreign investment. The inspiration for this move probably came from the abortive effort of E. H. Harriman, the American railway entrepreneur, to buy up the line from Port Arthur to Harbin that Japan had acquired from Russia, pour fresh capital into it, and use it as a link in a round-the-world transportation system. At first, when Japan was still at war and in need of money, Harriman's scheme received a favourable hearing in Tokyo; but its implications were all too clear – if Harriman got his way, Manchuria would ultimately emerge as an American economic dependency. So, despite Manchuria's impoverished condition, Japan under the influence of Baron Komura, who had negotiated the Portsmouth peace treaty, turned down Harriman's proposition. Subsequently Harriman approached the Russians with an offer to buy into the Trans-Siberian, but they too gave him a decisive negative.

At this point we must turn aside to note the resurgence of race antagonism in the United States that manifested itself first against the Chinese and then, more virulently on the Pacific coast, against the Japanese. Scattered incidents calculated to arouse resentment – a police raid on the Chinese quarter in Boston, Massachusetts, rude treatment meted out to visiting Chinese officials by the immigration authorities in San Francisco, and then, most insulting of all, the notorious segregation order of the San Francisco school board in October 1906 – brought stiff resistance from both China and Japan. The school board directive required that all Chinese, Japanese and Korean children within the city be separated from the rest and sent to a single school designated as the Oriental Public School. The exclusion treaty of 1894 which China had been coaxed into signing being due for renewal, demands arose for legislation prohibiting immigration of all Orientals who could be classified as labourers.

The noticeable number of Japanese entering the United States by way of Hawaii after 1898 sparked off the agitation. For instance, in

35 President Roosevelt with the plenipotentiaries attending the Portsmouth Conference on his yacht the *Mayflower* in Oyster Bay, 5 August 1905. From left to right: Witte, Baron Rosen, President Roosevelt, Baron Komura, Takahira.

1900 there were twelve thousand arrivals; and in 1905 the California legislature unanimously resolved that Japanese immigrants were 'immoral, intemperate, quarrelsome men bound to labour for a pittance'. Here was a new version of the 'yellow peril' which organized labour, apprehensive of the job market, heartily endorsed. The Japanese and Korean Exclusion League was started in this same year, while Japan was winning its impressive victories over Russia. Theodore Roosevelt understood the strain that this racial feeling would put upon the relations of the two countries, and he met it by negotiating with the Japanese government a gentleman's agreement whereby the latter would refuse passports to the mainland United States, and the President would secure the school board's consent to rescind its segregation order.

But Japan would not agree to withhold passports to Hawaii, which was an open portal to San Francisco; and the school board was not so easily managed as the President had hoped. Parallel anti-Oriental agitation developed in British Columbia, and the Canadian government experienced much the same embarrassment as the American in trying to cool the situation. School segregation moved to the state level in California in 1909, its proponents claiming that the 'pure maids' of the state were having to sit side by side with 'matured Japs, with their base minds, their lascivious thoughts'.[20] Strenuous efforts made by Mr Roosevelt with the help of the state governor finally defeated the bill, though by a margin of only four votes.

The Chinese response to these outrages took the form of organized boycotts of American-made goods and American shipping; a well-to-do merchant of Shanghai started the boycott in July 1905, and in spreading to other treaty ports it assumed rather formidable proportions. At least the American Asiatic Association thought so, and President Roosevelt demanded of the imperial government that it decree an end to the boycott. It was feared that a second Boxer uprising was in the making: five missionaries were slain in October, and anti-American demonstrations were sufficiently numerous to induce the American government to make preparations to dispatch an expeditionary force from the Philippines. While the Chinese gradually lost their enthusiasm, since Chinese merchants handling American goods were among the losers, the boycott seems to have been a departure from traditional xenophobia: it enlisted the sympathies of the student class, including Chinese Christians attending American schools in China, and of the Chinese in the United States.

Flushed with the pride of victory over a great European power, Japan was not to be brushed off as easily as the Chinese boycott. The Japanese government itself lost no time in protesting against the insults, and Roosevelt exercised all his powers of official and personal persuasion to calm the situation, realizing how this prejudice could destroy all the friendship of the previous years. 'The San Francisco mob bids fair,' he remarked, 'if not to embroil us with Japan, at any rate to arouse in Japan a feeling of rankling anger toward us that may at any time bear evil result; and the Japanese Jingoes are in their turn about as bad as ours.'[21] But the damage was done, to be followed, as we shall see, by many other wounds deliberately inflicted upon the Japanese. Theodore Roosevelt's gentleman's agreement erected a fine façade of Japanese-American goodwill, but anti-Japanese prejudice among the populace remained ready at hand for exploitation by the ultranationalist American press and politicians.

Roosevelt himself held Japan in high respect, ready to accord it recognition as a first-class power with a stake in Korea and Manchuria. But he was also bent on advancing the position of the United States as a world power, and the navy was in his eyes the instrument for attaining this end. To add to its prestige and to impress the Japanese with its strength, he sent a fleet of sixteen battleships on a round-the-world voyage in 1908; and, despite misgivings on how the Japanese would react to it, he sent it to Yokohama for a week's visit. The reception given it was extraordinarily cordial, proving the soundness of Roosevelt's judgment. Naturally the British ambassador was an interested observer, and he reported to the Foreign Office that the visit had been 'an unqualified success' having 'the effect our Allies wanted it to' and putting 'an end to all nonsensical war talk'.[22]

While open expressions of hostility were being manifested at the popular level in the United States, plans were being formulated by certain Americans holding official positions to put into practice Mr Conger's ideas regarding Manchuria. Since in their eyes this vast, sparsely settled country was 'contiguous' to the United States, America should have the controlling voice in determining its destiny. Manchuria, to use the phrase employed by Willard Straight, the most persistent of these men, was America's 'new West', a land to be developed by American private enterprise with the backing of the government. John Hay's 'open door' doctrine supplied justification for challenging Japan's claim to Manchuria as its sphere of influence, although Hay had meant only that the treaty port system of open trade be respected and made universal throughout China. Hay had not expected the powers to relinquish their several spheres of influence, nor had he conceived of an open door for capital investment. Straight and his associates put the emphasis on the latter, especially in terms of railways, although they wanted trade opportunities too. In other words, they intended to use the 'open door' as leverage on Japan, not only to force it to let go its hold but to convert Manchuria (eventually the Russian half too) into a United States sphere of influence. They relied on the power of American capital to secure monopoly control, and were not under any illusions as to what they were doing. They were playing in Straight's own words the 'Great Game of Empire'.

Willard Straight was an ambitious, compulsive young man from New York state who as a child had been allowed to have his own way. As an undergraduate at Cornell University he came under the influence of Professor Henry Morse Stephens, a tall Scotsman of Anglo-Indian parentage. Stephens headed the Cornell Kipling Club, and Willard saturated himself in the writings and ideas of Kipling. From this indoctrination it was an easy transition to the conviction that it was the duty of the West, particularly of America, to bring civilization to the Chinese. We should bear in mind that this passion for duty on the part of the 'superior' Anglo-Saxon was bred into the intellectual climate of Straight's generation. In the United States it was excited by the encounter with Spain.

Attracted to China and seeking adventure, Straight secured in 1901, the year of the Boxer uprising, an appointment in Peking with the Imperial Maritime Customs. There he became a close friend of J. O. P. Bland, an ambitious Irishman with important London banking connections. Bland was to prove one of Straight's most valuable allies. From the Customs Straight went to Korea as war correspondent for Reuters; and, paradoxically while on the side of Japan during the war, he conceived a bitter dislike and distrust of the Japanese. 'Insolent little brutes,' he called them in his diary, 'and yellow – that's what rubs one, the fact that a yellowman touches one – and that one must submit to his orders. It is maddening.'[23] This antipathy seems to have come from the short shrift Japanese army officers gave foreign correspondents trying to travel through the theatre of war. Straight had no trouble convincing himself of Japan's intention to expel the Western powers and take over China. Again we must remember that this was a widely shared opinion. Sir Robert Hart had expressed the same thought in 1895, though in more moderate language.

As time passed and Straight in 1906 was appointed consul-general in Mukden, he found influential friends and allies in private life, in journalism and in government circles who were disposed to thwart Japan and make an American preserve out of Manchuria. One of the first of these was T'ang Shao-yi, the Chinese governor of Fengtien province who had granted Japan monopoly railway rights in South Manchuria. But T'ang was ready to work the other side of the street: a Manchurian Bank financed by American capital, to be made fiscal agent of the Chinese provincial government and given various concessions to develop the country; a railway to run from Hsinmintun to Fakumen, later to be extended to Tsitsihar, where it would intersect the Russian-owned Chinese Eastern Railway, and on to Aigun on the Siberian border. This was a parallel line to the South Manchurian Railway (SMR), meant to undercut the Japanese. Straight took the bait offered by the bank proposition. While T'ang's motive had been to use the United States as a buffer against Japan, Straight's was 'the White Man's Burden... to save China from herself as much as from the predatory peoples from the East and North. Save her . . . that we altruists may reap the profits of her development ourselves, for . . . that, is it not, is what our philanthropy means?'

Through Bland's initiative the charter for the Hsinmintun-Fakumen railway went to a British company, much to Straight's satisfaction. This line 'will threaten the Japanese strategic position and place a splendid line of communication along the Japanese flank and within easy reach of the Russians whose activities in Mongolia have already aroused the apprehensions of their late, and possible future enemies.'[24]

Among Straight's many other friends were George Marvin, an adventurous young Harvard man who set up an anti-Japanese news bureau in Mukden and ran it as part of the consulate; and Thomas F. Millard, Far Eastern correspondent of the *New York Herald* and also president of the American Association of China. Millard was a candid believer in the government taking a hand in opening new markets in Asia for American industry, and he got the ear of William Howard Taft while Taft was visiting in Shanghai. It was an open secret that Taft would be the next occupant of the White House, and a speech he made in Shanghai was all that Millard and the American businessmen of that city could desire. Subsequently Taft got a thorough briefing on Manchuria as the key to economic and political dominance over China, and on the need for checkmating Japan. The 'open door' was the cover for these forward policies.

Two other key men were actively involved in this game. One was F. M. Huntington Wilson, who had served in the legation in Tokyo; the other was William Phillips, who had been with the Peking legation. In opening the new Far Eastern Division of the State Department in March 1908, these men appeared as advocates of Straight's crusade, preferring charges against Japan and urging a forward policy upon the Secretary of State. Their one influential opponent was Rockhill, the original author of Hay's notes. Rockhill had proposed remission of the Boxer indemnity over and above the cost of the relief expedition, and advocated using the funds to finance the education of Chinese students in American universities. But Wilson and Phillips endorsed a proposal by T'ang Shao-yi to divert the funds as a basis for financing the Manchurian Bank, which would then enter upon a development programme aimed at the Japanese.

In July 1907 Japan had agreed with Russia on their respective spheres in Manchuria, each pledging itself not to seek concessions in the sphere of the other. While 'secret', this agreement came to the attention of the Secretary of State, Elihu Root, whom early the next year the Japanese ambassador, Baron Takahira, approached in the hope of winning a similar accord with the United States or at least of getting something that would show American goodwill. Naturally Straight and his friends opposed any pact of friendship with Japan, but Root and Theodore Roosevelt were no advocates of an aggressive policy in Manchuria. They were, however, caught between a desire to be conciliatory toward Japan and a recognition that they could not go so far as to give that country a 'free hand' in Manchuria. The sticking-point was the issue of China's 'territorial integrity' and 'sovereignty' over Manchuria. Neither Japan nor Russia regarded these phrases as real, although they permitted the Chinese to continue exercising the functions of provincial government in this region. In the *entente* arrived at by Root and Takahira in November 1908 no allusion to Manchuria appears. The two parties agreed on their mutual desire to maintain the 'existing *status quo*' in the region of the Pacific Ocean and on the principle of equal opportunity for commerce and industry in China. The agreement got a cordial reception in both countries, but it was still possible for men like Straight to fish in the troubled waters of Manchuria.

China proper, however, furnished even deeper waters in which to fish, and Straight and his New York and Washington friends came to believe in 1909 that opportunity was knocking at their door in the Yangtze valley. A British-French-German syndicate was proposing to make a loan to the imperial government for the purpose of building two railways out of Hankow: one to the south, the other to the west. This was known as the Hukuang loan, covering the provinces of Hupeh and Hunan. Four New York banks organized themselves in June as the American Group and, allied with the new Taft administration in Washington, demanded a one-quarter share in this project. 'The path of empire,' wrote Huntington Wilson for *Harper's Weekly*, 'lay along the railroad.' Railway building in China would provide the needed outlet for the dreaded surplus of American industry; and the administration regarded admission to the Hukuang loan as a test of the vitality of the open door. Moreover, as Huntington Wilson put it, the bankers' patriotism was at issue: it was their duty to America to make available in China the 'countless commercial opportunities' arising out of the internal development of that country. [25]

The Hukuang loan never materialized – the British did not want intruders in their sphere and refused to co-operate. But the loan brought a resurgence of Chinese xenophobia: hostility to all foreign investments and renewed opposition to the Ch'ing dynasty for giving the country away to foreigners. This was the 'rights recovery' movement, pointing to revolution and overthrow of the dynasty.

From this ill-fated project Willard Straight managed to turn attention back to Manchuria. Straight's new scheme was to build a long railroad from Chinchow to Aigun, supplanting his previous scheme which had come to nothing. The American Group supported him, and the administration elaborated upon the plan by a proposition to 'neutralize' the railways of Manchuria: Russia and Japan to transfer ownership of their respective lines to an international banking group. Straight, in a personal visit to St Petersburg, tried hard to attract Russian interest; and with Russia on the American side, he felt confident he could coerce Japan into surrender. Ironically these studied efforts to shepherd all the powers – Britain, France and Germany included – under the banner of the American open door led not merely to rejection but to a second Russo-Japanese agreement in 1910, dividing Manchuria between them without so much as paying lip-service to the mystical phrase of the open door. The 'American peril' – the fear lest the United States win economic and financial supremacy over the rest of the world – had begun to haunt the European mind at least as far back as the war with Spain; and the 'dollar diplomacy' of the Taft government convinced the powers that the peril was real.

Straight and his supporters made one more effort to 'save China' and at the same time reap the profit, especially in Manchuria. Straight's phrases reflected the attitudes of President Taft, Secretary Knox and Huntington Wilson, but *not* those of Theodore Roosevelt; and they defined the policy of the American government. The United States, Straight liked to say, had a 'great responsibility' to finish the tasks 'vital to the regeneration of China and most essential to placing her on her feet'. Roosevelt tried to stop Taft and Knox from pursuing this will-o'-the-wisp, but without success. The American position in Manchuria, he argued, was untenable and would only lead to more trouble with Japan. As for the 'open door', it too was a fantasy, certain to be ignored by any power to whom it was an inconvenience. [26]

Straight's new enthusiasm in 1911 was for an international banking loan to the Manchu régime, designed ostensibly to reform and stabilize Chinese currency. To this end China should be made to accept an American financial adviser after the manner of the Caribbean republics and of the British protectorate over Egypt. Russia and Japan both interpreted this project as a cloak for American economic penetration of Manchuria, and they were correct. Secretary Knox himself said as much to the French ambassador. The United States, he admitted, 'in reality desired to use this sum for the building of railways and the penetration of Manchuria'.[27] Pursuing the ambitions of the deceased Harriman, Knox aspired to box in the Japanese SMR with American lines that would then launch rate wars forcing Japan to yield. It was the same sort of ruthless and wasteful competition in railway construction familiar to American railway building during the nineteenth century, conducted with little serious consideration for economic advantage but rather as a purely speculative enterprise on the part of the American Banking group, aided and abetted by the American government.

Although having scant respect for the Ch'ing dynasty, which they knew was permeated with corruption, none of these men recognized the gathering forces of revolution nor were they prepared to cope with it. Outbreaks led by the provincial mandarins against the Hukuang loan of 1909 were the symptoms, followed by another rebellion in Szechuan province in October 1911 which signalled the start of the revolution. With this event the proposed currency loan and kindred projects for 'saving' China by shoring up the decadent dynasty came to a dead stop.

6 Revolution in China, friction with Japan

Riots, attacks on missionaries and many other expressions of animosity toward foreigners had not been wanting in China since the
humiliation of 1842. The Ch'ing dynasty, as we have seen, was by
that time already on its death march; the Taiping rebels, who
engaged in massive civil war for its overthrow, hung on for twelve
years. Its concessions to the foreign powers, and the monstrous
indemnities the latter continued to impose, identified this alien
Manchu dynasty with the barbarian enemy. Like its predecessors, it
was fated to go. Among the mandarins, such as Li Hung-chang, a
'self-strengthening' movement had taken hold: a cautious willingness
to accept certain Western material benefits, notably railways, if
Chinese culture was to be saved from extinction. 'If one knows
oneself and knows one's opposite number, in a hundred battles one
will have a hundred victories' – an ancient adage invoked by Li
about the time when the *tsungli yamen* was established.[1] China was
still the world – the Confucian world.

The nation (*kuo*) was a foreign conception, a political unit among
other political units, and therefore destructive of traditional Chinese
values. But as the foreign powers grew more demanding, the instinct
of self-preservation compelled the Chinese to turn to this unwelcome
idea. The 'new China' of the patriotic societies which came out into
the open after the Boxer uprising centred on the 'rights recovery'
movement of Sun Yat-sen, and made its unofficial début in 1905,
when Sun issued his Three Principles of the People. This was a
manifesto of revolution, calling for a complete overhauling of Chinese
society on the basis of mass democracy. And 'the day will arrive,'
concluded Sun, 'when we look over our shoulder and find Europe
and America lagging far behind.'

Sun instigated numerous revolutionary outbreaks, but he was not
a party to the revolt in Szechuan which developed into revolution
and forced the Ch'ing dynasty into exile in 1912. Provincial governors, their officials and the local gentry upon whom they depended
joined in repudiating the central government which had betrayed
them to the foreigners; and the Peiyang army, which controlled the
north, put its commanding general, Yüan Shih-k'ai, at the head of
the new régime in Peking. Meanwhile in the south Sun Yat-sen had
organized a revolutionary national party, the Kuomintang, which

36 Dr Sun Yat-sen. Photograph taken in 1923.

held a national assembly in Nanking; but, hoping to hold the country together, Sun resigned in favour of Yüan and induced his followers to elect the latter president of the Republic of China.

All of this happened within the space of a few months, but the real revolution was still seven years away. On the surface Yüan emerged as the strong man of China, outraging republicans by his personal rule and displaying an inclination to found a dynasty of his own. From this ambition he was forced to retreat, and at his death in June 1916 only the shell of a central authority survived in Peking. Power in the provinces devolved upon the local warlords – sometimes civil governors, sometimes military men, but whose successes in any event depended upon their ability to hire and maintain mercenaries. The era of the warlords lasted into the late 1920s; but in the meantime a new revolutionary outbreak occurred in Peking, sparked by student indignation against Japan and against the Western powers who, it was believed, had delivered China into Japanese hands. This outbreak became known as the 'May Fourth Movement' of 1919; since it carried overtones of lasting revolution, we shall return to it later.

37 Revolution in China, 1912. A Republican soldier cuts off the pigtail (the ancient Chinese symbol of servitude) from another Chinese.

Throughout 1912, the first year of the revolution, Willard Straight continued to be representative of American policy, and in Peking he acted as agent of the American banking group. Instinctively he strove to shore up the bankrupt dynasty: only foreign money could do that, and only Great Britain could contribute enough to make it practicable. But the British government would not underwrite the loan, and neither the Manchus nor Yüan Shih-k'ai, whose financial needs were as great as theirs, could get the kind of foreign aid that might keep them going. Straight's goal was a six-power consortium, including Russia and Japan and, of course, the United States, that would have a common interest in preserving the central government. The alternative in his mind was China's complete break-up into spheres of interest, Russia and Japan extracting the greatest advantages. Straight's programme for an international trusteeship was a departure from his original belief that the United States could be made the dominant power in China, but the crisis in 1912 forced him to modify his plans.

Soon after the advent of Woodrow Wilson to power in the United States in 1912, the American banking group took its case direct to Washington, saying that if it was to pour money into China it would need government backing. This, however, the administration declined to provide. But there was another side to the matter which the bankers had not taken into account: no sooner was Yüan Shih-k'ai made President of China than his army mutinied for want of pay, and the provincial leaders refused to come to his aid. For him to accept an international trusteeship, even if offered, was politically impossible. It meant total surrender to the foreigners. To the provincial mandarinate and its several armies who had already broken with Yüan this was intolerable.

Superficially, but only superficially, Woodrow Wilson broke with the dollar diplomacy of his predecessor. He snubbed the New York banking group, not even deigning to give them a reply but going direct to the newspapers with the announcement of his refusal. The New York group filled the image of 'Wall Street', a ready target for Democratic Party politicians. But other financiers, jealous of the New York monopoly, took heart: the President, they learned, meant to open the door wide for investment opportunities. Lesser fry could compete for the favours of China, and the government would give them its blessing. It only meant to checkmate the particular group promoted by Willard Straight and Huntington Wilson. Woodrow Wilson executed two other gestures dear to the American heart: he announced that his policy would be to act *alone* and not in accord with an international body; and he proceeded to recognize the Republic of China under Yüan Shih-k'ai. Americans could take pride in their independence of Europe and in their President's generosity in extending the hand of friendship to a 'sister republic'.

The very capable German ambassador to Washington, Count von Bernstorff, saw through these moves:

Like all statesmen here [he reported], Wilson is sometimes forced to play to the gallery, whether with altruistic circumlocutions or with digs in the ribs of such unpopular fellow-citizens as J. P. Morgan.... Mr Wilson is already preparing to consolidate the American position in China by recognizing the Republic, and other American bankers are giving signs of being ready to lend money to China, even though the Republic is not prepared to act as guardian in an administrative capacity.[2]

The sequel demonstrates Bernstorff's acuteness. Business and religion were natural allies in Wilson's mind. China was 'the market for which statesmen as well as merchants must plan and play their game of competition, the market to which diplomacy, and if need be power, must make an open way'.[3] These were the words with which Wilson had originally defined his conception of the 'open door'. Wilson got his education in Chinese matters from the missionaries, in particular from the career missionary-editor, S. I. Woodbridge, who was his cousin, and from Bishop J. W. Bashford, who knew Peking well; and in his mind and even more in that of Bryan, the Secretary of State, his administration must be represented in Peking by an evangelical Christian. He was disappointed that John R. Mott, the head of the YMCA, would not accept the post, but in Paul S. Reinsch, the son of a Lutheran clergyman and a professor at the University of Wisconsin who had written on Far Eastern affairs, he found the perfect minister.

Reinsch naïvely believed the Chinese had actually chosen the United States as their model republic, and that therefore it was his duty to give the men in Yüan Shih-k'ai's government the benefit of his advice. From his book, *An American Diplomat in China*, we get no notion of the fragility of Yüan's régime, which the provincial mandarins defied; and when it collapsed in 1916, Reinsch was optimistic that China, under American guidance, would become more genuinely 'republican'. Apparently oblivious of the growing power of the warlords, his sovereign remedy for China was industrialization, and to that end he sought to open up opportunities for American corporations.

The Bethlehem Steel Corporation was eager to supply China with warships and to build a base for them on the coast of Fukien, the financing to be done through a new bond issue by the admittedly bankrupt government. The Standard Oil companies were pursuing the Chinese market for kerosene, and they too received the gratuitous backing of the American minister. Foremost among Reinsch's projects, however, was a thirty-million-dollar administrative loan which he believed would put Yüan's régime on its feet. A Boston investment house advanced a million, but other American bankers hung back pending a guarantee from their government, which President Wilson would not give. But in 1915 Bethlehem Steel, in co-operation with the Electric Boat Company of Connecticut, returned to its original cause in an offer to build submarines for China. Retired American naval officers had a hand in this scheme, a former naval attaché in Peking acting as agent for Bethlehem and a former lieutenant supervising the instruction of some thirty young Chinese whom the Electric Boat Company brought to its plant for training. In these

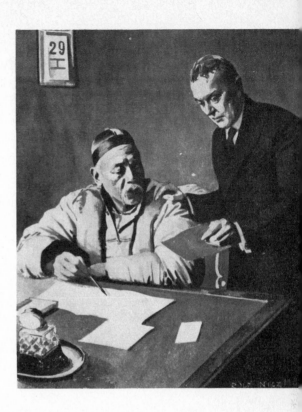

38 Dr G. E. Morrison, the political adviser of the Chinese Republic, and Yüan Shih-k'ai, its first President, 1912. Drawing in the *Illustrated London News*.

relationships we see the beginnings of the industrial-military complex. When Yüan's régime fell in 1916, Bethlehem turned its attention to the warlords, but they too were put off when the United States government, having entered the war in Europe, took up the slack in the company's productive capacity.

While the Americans were vainly using high pressure sales methods on the Chinese, the Japanese were taking advantage of the opportunities provided them by the European war. Occupation of Kiaochow Bay in November 1914 and of all the German islands north of the Equator gave the Japanese naval preponderance in the western Pacific. Then in January 1915 they levied upon Yüan Shih-k'ai a series of twenty-one demands calculated to make Japan the overlord of China. Fukien province, Shantung and Manchuria were to be special spheres of interest, with room for deeper penetration into China. Bethlehem Steel's obvious desire to obtain a foothold on the Fukien coast had put the Japanese on the alert, Shantung was Japan's war legacy from Germany, while Manchuria had been a special object of Japanese interest ever since the war with Russia. Then there was a final set of demands requiring Yüan to accept Japanese advisers in political, financial and military matters, to share control of the municipal police, and to import at least half of his war munitions from Japan.

Considering the defiance of the various provincial warlords and the melting away of Yüan's army, these notorious demands and the reactions of the United States to them contain a large element of unreality. As we have seen, to sustain his rule Yüan had to have unlimited support from the outside, but it is questionable whether even Japan was prepared to go that far. Several months of negotiation followed, Japan retreating part of the way on paper but actually making little, if any, advance against the growing anarchy of its massive neighbour. Reinsch, who imagined China to be the reincarnation of the American Republic, regarded Japan's aggressions as a challenge to the United States and wanted to respond accordingly. But the Wilson administration preferred to temporize. Secretary Bryan acknowledged that 'territorial contiguity' created 'special relations' between Japan and Shantung, South Manchuria and East Mongolia; and the debate was terminated with a formal note reiterating the platitudes of 'treaty rights', 'the political or territorial integrity' of China, and 'the international policy . . . commonly known as the open door policy'.

Anxious to conciliate the United States and to capitalize on Bryan's admission that geography entitled Japan to claim a special relationship to parts of the mainland, the Japanese in the summer of 1917 sent the very personable Viscount Ishii to Washington in the hope of winning American goodwill and encouragement to go ahead in China. From Britain and France the Japanese had already obtained commitments relating to Shantung and the Pacific Islands. Ishii drew the analogy of the relation of the United States to Latin America under the Monroe Doctrine, and he hoped the Wilson administration would see the point and grant that Japan had a similar paramount interest in China. But after much sparring over terms he emerged with another ambiguous agreement reaffirming the traditional phrases and putting no meaning into the connection between 'territorial contiguity' and 'special relations'. Nothing of value emerged; ideas on each side remained fixed, and since the United States stressed its 'open door policy' while Japan stressed its 'special position', the net result was to show that there was no basis for mutual agreement.

In the following summer, American bankers having shied away from political loans to China, Wilson reversed his previous attitude toward international bankers. He now wanted a new international banking consortium, on the theory that it would encourage American bankers to come forward in a chance to share the risks; but the bankers were unresponsive, and Wilson's China policies were reduced to the hollow phrases which he had inherited from the past. Such foreign money as China obtained during the war came from Japan.

For different reasons the United States, Japan and the weak Peking régime itself all wanted China to declare war on Germany. The *casus belli* was ludicrous: without any stake in the outcome of the German submarine warfare in the distant Atlantic, China would advance 'the peace of the world' by joining the United States against it. Minister Reinsch worked assiduously for the cause, regarding it as a demonstration of Chinese willingness to follow the American lead; Japan did likewise as a means of showing that it, not America, was the chosen leader of the Orient. The northern warlords, led by Tuan Chi-jui, saw in a break with Germany the means of tightening their grip internally against the southern-dominated Kuomintang; and if they got a war loan from the United States, as Reinsch hoped they would, they meant to use it for this purpose. From Washington they got advice, but no money; from Tokyo they got money and arms enough to render them subservient to Japan; from the Kuomintang they got defiance and the setting up of a separate régime centred on Canton. The Japanese succeeded in establishing civil government in Shantung, and in September 1918 Peking agreed that they would inherit the German rights in that province and be given a concession to build new railways there and in Manchuria and Mongolia. As Woodrow Wilson himself remarked, 'Japan certainly has China very much in her grasp.' [4] But this was due as much to Chinese venality as to Japanese ambition, and American diplomacy was moving into the absurd position of trying to save China from itself.

Contemporaneously a complicated situation developed in eastern Siberia, bringing Japanese-American mistrust further into focus. Fears of the Russian Bolsheviks taking over Vladivostok in 1917 and operating the Trans-Siberian Railway for the benefit of Germany were sufficient to induce Britain and France to advocate a Japanese occupation. Six hundred thousand tons of supplies were tied up in Vladivostok awaiting shipment. Moreover, a force of fifty thousand Czech soldiers was known to be somewhere in Russia seeking to make its way to Vladivostok for transfer back to the western front in

Europe. Japan was the natural power for the occupation and for the protection of the railway; and after much hesitation it took over the city in April 1918.

Sceptical of Japanese intentions, President Wilson refused to join in this move although he had the opportunity and indeed was urged to do so by his advisers as well as by the British government. Finally in August a belated American occupation, comprising seven thousand men from the Philippines, took place; but the Japanese continued expanding their forces so that by October they had seventy thousand strung out along the railway as far west as Lake Baikal. Obviously the American intervention was not merely too late, but too weak, to thwart a Japanese plan to absorb eastern Siberia. Japan supported a White Russian régime under Admiral Kolchak, apparently gambling upon Kolchak's winning a victory over the Bolsheviks. In that event Kolchak would have to continue relying upon Japan; but the Bolsheviks turned the tables on all three parties, overthrowing Kolchak and setting up the communist Far Eastern Republic at Vladivostok. The Americans were the first to give up this ill-starred intervention, evacuating the port in April 1920; they were followed by the Japanese two years later. For both countries the intervention was a total fiasco, but it left bruised feelings between the Americans and the Japanese.

It was during the Paris Peace Conference of 1919 and its aftermath that friction between America and Japan broke into the open. A new version of the 'yellow peril' had made its appearance in California just before the war; Japanese immigrants, it was claimed, were buying agricultural land at a rate that would eventually put them in control of the state's farm-lands; and to check this alleged peril the state legislature enacted an anti-alien land law. Indignant at this and at other exasperating forms of discrimination in the United States and other countries, notably in Australia, Japan seized the opening furnished by President Wilson's enthusiasm for the League of Nations to make known its wish for a racial equality clause in the League Covenant. Like Theodore Roosevelt in earlier years, Wilson in 1913 had exerted himself to get the California legislation rescinded, but to no avail. Strident politicians like the state governor, Hiram Johnson, thwarted him; and when Japan in 1919 identified the League with the cause of racial equality, Wilson faced a similar dilemma. The Australian Prime Minister threatened a flint-like resistance, and the Japanese having more practical gains in mind gave up on this issue.

39 The Japanese delegates at the Paris Peace Conference, 1919.

But Japan was now a first-class power, the leader in East Asia and in actual possession of Shantung province and of all the German islands north of the Equator. A wartime agreement with Britain had pledged Japan's retention of these islands after the war. But at Paris the American delegation raised objections; on principle Wilson opposed colonial acquisitions, but his advisers also educated him in the strategy of the western Pacific. One of them, Breckinridge Long, a career officer in the State Department whose experience went back to the Russo-Japanese war, took a position against both the Japanese- and the British-held islands. They were 'a constant menace to the United States and its dominant position' in the Pacific. Long was prepared to resort to bad faith in order to get the islands for the United States: he would have them returned to Germany, who was in turn to be required to hand them over to the United States. This, however, was too strong medicine, and in the end the islands were left in British and Japanese hands respectively as 'Class C' mandates, trust territories under the League of Nations.

40 Wellington Koo, the Chinese Minister to the United States and head of the Chinese delegation at the Paris Peace Conference.

Shantung was the prime cause of American-Japanese friction, and the compromise finally reached over it brought disappointment to Japan, a bitterness in the United States so great that it was a major factor in the country's refusal to join the League of Nations, and a fresh revolutionary outburst in China. China's paper war on Germany paid off handsomely: it opened the doors in Paris for a separate Chinese delegation eager to plead its case, and the delegation was so made up as to disguise the internal schism in China and to fulfil the dream of Minister Reinsch and others that America was the chosen defender of China against an aggressive Japan.

There were two heads of the Chinese delegation, both in their thirties and zealous defenders of the 'New China'. V. K. Wellington Koo was a former protegé of Yüan Shih-k'ai, and a student of John Bassett Moore, the distinguished American authority on international law at Columbia University. At this time he was minister to the United States, representing the Peking régime. C. T. Wang, a Yale University product, came from Canton with the original intention of diverting American interest in favour of the Kuomintang; but in Paris Wang and Koo presented a united front. Through Reinsch the Chinese delegation was further reinforced by two able advisers, one American, the other British, who had seen long service in Peking.

The first was William W. Willoughby of Johns Hopkins University, the second was George E. Morrison, correspondent for the London *Times*. In a word, the Chinese delegation was unusually able and superior in quality to the Japanese; and the Chinese were conditioned to look upon America, and Wilson in particular, as their champion. With Wilson's help Japan would be checked, and a new and better régime would emerge to unify China.

Pointing to Tsingtao as the best harbour on the China coast and to its railway to Tsinan, which commanded the entire trade of North China, Koo asked the American delegation in Paris to obtain direct restitution of the German rights in Shantung to China. The agreement of 1915 with Japan had been made under duress, and the part of Tsingtao which the Japanese wanted reserved for themselves comprised the vital business section. Indirect restitution would be objectionable: Chinese pride was heightened over this issue, and practical considerations were also at stake. Wilson understood and sympathized with the gravity of the Chinese desire, and he realized too that the matter was in his hands. But it behooved the United States to tread carefully; Japanese sensibilities were also involved. As Colonel House told the President, 'We cannot meet Japan in her desires as to land and immigration, and unless we make some concessions in regard to her sphere of influence in the East, trouble is sure sooner or later to come.'[5] But only House appreciated the Japanese side; all the other members of the American delegation, including the 'experts', were avowedly pro-Chinese.

A crisis was now at hand. The Italian delegation had defied Wilson and gone home, and if Japan followed suit the peace conference was likely to break up. Such was Wilson's conviction. So on 30 April 1919 the terms which the Japanese delegation had drafted were incorporated in the treaty. They were to the effect that Germany renounced in favour of Japan all its rights, title and privileges in Shantung and in the railways and other properties which the Germans had developed. Other powers too had special claims which had to be met; and as for the United States, it possessed a stranglehold at the time over its own special sphere, the region of the Caribbean. None other than Woodrow Wilson had pushed American national interest in this region to its peak.

Nevertheless there was a thunderous reaction to Japan's claims to Shantung. The pro-Chinese members of the American delegation in Paris resigned, as did Minister Reinsch, and a storm of vituperative speeches broke loose in the United States Senate. Such words as 'immoral', 'rape', 'international grand larceny', 'monstrous', were favourites in the rhetoric of the senators, especially of the Republicans who discovered they could make dynamite of the Shantung issue. Alarmed by these outbursts, Japan softened its position by publicly denying its intention to utilize Tsingtao as an exclusive concession; but Wilson too realized he had made himself vulnerable, and so he declared his 'grave concern' and asked Japan to give 'immediate assurance' of withdrawal from Shantung. To the Japanese this meant complete surrender, and so the dispute over Shantung came to a halt at a dangerous stage. As things turned out, Japan became a party to the peace treaty and a member of the League of Nations, but not the United States nor China.

While the senators were fuming against Japan's aggressions and making political capital out of Wilson's 'mistakes' to the end of defeating the Versailles treaty, the revolutionary 'May Fourth Movement' broke out in China. The predicament of that country stood out in stark contrast to the fiction of its 'territorial integrity and independence'. The bureaucratic régime, the successor to Yüan Shih-k'ai in Peking, pretended to be sovereign over the whole of China; and the foreign powers in turn pretended that it was sovereign. All the treaty powers maintained diplomatic contact, their envoys residing in the Legation Quarter of Peking, a compound protected by armed guards from the various nations and barred to all Chinese not provided with the proper credentials. The same was true of the several International Settlements (notably Shanghai), concession areas and leased territories.

The Peking government depended upon the foreign-controlled Maritime Customs Inspectorate, upon the salt tax, and upon such contributions as the many local warlords who were the real power in the provinces chose to make. All these revenues were mortgaged in one way or another, pledged to meet the interest and amortization charges of the many foreign loans and indemnities inherited from the past. The customs rates, which were the surest source of revenue, were fixed by the treaty powers and could not be changed. The Peking bureaucracy on its part was improvident, surviving by a hand-to-mouth existence and constantly begging for more money from the foreign powers. During the war Japan alone had been the source of funds, so that it should occasion no surprise that the Japanese felt a special interest in their huge and unmanageable pro-tegé. Armed with extraterritorial rights and privileges, the nationals of the treaty powers kept their own law courts and post offices, so that any Chinese who disputed with a foreigner had to submit to the jurisdiction of that foreigner's court. Foreign warships patrolled China's inland waters, notably the Yangtze and the Peiho, and foreign troops could be summoned at will when needed. In sum, China was a mere geographical expression, as Metternich once said of Italy.

Intelligence received from Paris that Shantung had been handed over to Japan set off the May Fourth Movement, Japan being already planted in the Chinese mind as the principal enemy. The twenty-one demands had done that, and 7 May, the anniversary of the 1915 ultimatum, was commemorated annually as National Humiliation Day. In 1919, however, it was three days early: the consequence of violence and mass arrests arising out of a student demonstration in Peking. Compounding this existing antagonism toward Japan was the knowledge that only a few months previously the Peking government had played into Japanese hands: in return for a secret loan it had 'gladly agreed' to Japanese occupation and control of Shantung; and moreover, by its attempt to suppress the demonstration the government as good as confessed that it was pro-Japanese; at least that was the view taken by the students and the Peking populace. An inner group of warlords known as the Anfu clique controlled the government, behaving in a manner characteristic of the fallen Ch'ing dynasty.

The demonstrating students came from the National University of Peking, founded since the 1911 revolution and the recognized centre of the reform movement. Their manifesto, written in the vernacular (*pai-hua*) rather than in classical Chinese (*wen-yen*), insisted that the loss of Shantung would finish off China: 'Once the integrity of her territory is destroyed, China will soon be annihilated. . . . This is the last chance for China in her life and death struggle.'[6] So the May Fourth movement, which really dated from the indignation over the Japanese twenty-one demands, brought to the fore the older 'rights recovery' movement of Sun Yat-sen. To break Japan's grip was the immediate object; but the ultimate goal was to remodel the Chinese political and social structure, obliterating the literature, thought and system of worship of Confucian China and appropriating the democratic, nationalist and socialist ideas of the West. The 'unequal treaties' (a phrase which now became current) would be repudiated, the Western powers (but not Western influences) would be ejected, and China be made mistress in her own house. Pre-Boxer xenophobia underwent a metamorphosis: Chinese nationalists fiercely resented the century-old privileges of the Western powers, but to rid the country of these oppressions they turned to the nation state system of the West and gave ear to the advice of European and American reformers, liberals and socialists. To this end the Kuomintang, a revolutionary conglomerate of nationalists and communists with roots in Canton but with headquarters until 1916 in Tokyo, solidified in 1919 into a single party determined to destroy the old régime and its symbol of power, the Peking government.

As in earlier Chinese upheavals, population pressure correlates with the May Fourth movement. Peking doubled its population in the four years from 1919 to 1923; a rising number of half-starved, landless peasants drifted into the cities or joined the private armies of the warlords who forged ahead at this time. Ten major civil wars occurred in China over a seven-year period between 1915 and 1922. Furthermore, the Chinese revolution was contemporary with similar upheavals in the West – in Russia of course in particular, but also in Germany, Austria, Hungary and other European countries. Mexico initiated its socialist revolution in 1917.

But the unique feature of May Fourth was the student movement, animated by the large numbers who had absorbed a Western type of education and who were prepared to seize the leadership. 'Chinese studies as the fundamental structure, Western studies for practical use.' This was their watchword, repeated with growing emphasis since the turn of the century. Thus a literary revolution had been virtually consummated by this time: the abandonment of Confucian teaching and of classical Chinese, which were known only to a small minority, in favour of the vernacular expressed through numerous books, magazines and speeches reflecting Western political and social ideas.

At Peking university were, among others, Hu Shih, a disciple of the American educator John Dewey, and Ch'en Tu-hsiu, an admirer of the English philosopher-socialist Bertrand Russell. Hu Shih had studied in the United States for seven years, and his professor arrived on the eve of May Fourth, remaining in China for two years, delivering outstanding lectures to large student audiences, and travelling extensively throughout the country. Dewey's subsequent writings in America showed a grasp of Chinese culture and social problems far superior to that of men like Rockhill or Reinsch who were incapable of taking off their American spectacles. Dewey flatly declared the ideas of such men irrelevant, criticized the teaching of history for its being made to fit into the mould of one-sided nationalism, and queried whether the nation state as matured in the West had not begun its period of decline.

Many other Chinese had studied in the United States – some fifteen hundred in American schools in the year 1915, for example – and it seems likely that John Dewey's ability to comprehend China derived from his contacts with his Chinese students at Columbia University, notably with Hu Shih, who was foremost in bringing about the literary revolution. Surprisingly, however, Japan stands first in importance in influencing the May Fourth Movement. As early as 1906 Japanese schools were educating thirteen thousand Chinese and, spread over the whole period, forty-one per cent. of Chinese students going abroad chose Japan. Students returning from that country – both Chou En-lai and Chiang Kai-shek were among them – supplied the extremist and militant leadership for May Fourth. But Chou had previously studied in France, as had Ch'en Tu-hsiu, one of the founders of Chinese communism. Mao Tse-tung, while not going abroad, was an avid student of English and French works; and French influence found its mark in anarchist and guild socialist doctrines.

Bertrand Russell's influence on the Chinese revolution, as measured by the number of his student readers, was greater than that of John Dewey. Russell came in 1920 at the instance of Chinese radicals and, having been to Moscow just previously and seen Bolshevik doctrines of communism and pacifism through rose-coloured glasses, concluded that Russia was a better teacher for China than the capitalist West. Like many of his contemporaries, Russell fancied that industrialization opened the road to world peace and, with a definite set of panaceas to offer, he left a more lasting mark on the Chinese student mentality than Dewey's stereotype of 'parliamentary democracy'.

From the initial incident in Peking, demonstrations and strikes spread rapidly to other Chinese cities, notably to Tientsin and Shanghai, which latter city soon became the headquarters of the student revolution. Merchants and urban workers supported the students against mass arrests, and the trend toward communism continued. But in terms of tangible results the May Fourth Movement ended in a blind alley. It succeeded in preventing the Peking government from signing the Treaty of Versailles, but it was unprepared for a full-scale revolution. Warlords continued to prevail in the northern capital and throughout the provinces, while the Kuomintang as a coalition of nationalists and communists maintained its foothold at Canton in the south.

7 Chinese nationalism and
the Manchurian tinderbox

The central government at Peking, declared the American minister, John Van Antwerp MacMurray, in August 1926, was a diplomatic fiction with not even a 'plausible claim to being a legitimately constituted government . . . a mere agency of whatever military factions control it . . . a pawn used in a fantastic game being played among military rivals having no loyalties and no principles . . . a local political organization' like those at Canton and Shanghai, differing from them only in that it enjoyed recognition by foreign governments whose treaty rights it was both unable and unwilling to respect. The Chinese people themselves regarded it with shame and derision; throughout the country there was an unmistakable trend toward decentralization, an abandonment of even the idea of a central government.

The practical reason for keeping up the front of diplomatic recognition, MacMurray argued, no longer existed. 'It is as though we had taken to the Central Government as a life raft in the political shipwreck of the Chinese Republic; and that raft, its buoyancy lost now, is no longer keeping us afloat. To keep it afloat we are swimming, but despite this, it must soon drag us down.' MacMurray was a career diplomat with a background of experience in China, a recognized authority on the treaty system but without the illusions or evangelizing zeal of men like Rockhill, Willard Straight or Paul Reinsch. At the time, there was an international conference on the Chinese tariff in session at Peking, its objective being to restore to the Chinese the control over their own customs of which the treaties had deprived them. A commission on extraterritoriality was also scheduled, a reduction or elimination of the legal immunities of foreigners being the intended objective. But if, as MacMurray insisted, China had no central government, such measures were impracticable. He and the other envoys were relying upon their various consular officers to do business with the local authorities who had the power and the responsibility; the foreign ministry in Peking was factitious, hence they were disposed to ignore it. Accordingly MacMurray urged Washington to issue a formal statement withdrawing recognition from the Peking régime.[1]

But the recommendation embarrassed the administration in Washington: the factual situation which MacMurray described and to which the Secretary of State, Frank B. Kellogg, took no exception, was contrary to the proclaimed policies and ideals of the United States regarding China. To adopt the recommendation would be to confess failure. The myth of 'the sovereignty, the independence, and the territorial and administrative integrity of China' had to be preserved. These words had been written into the Nine Power Treaty of 1921, one of the major accomplishments of American diplomacy at the Washington Conference. The United States at this conference had persuaded eight other treaty powers, including Japan, to accept its principles and to promote the cause of China, although MacMurray's analysis was as authentic for 1921 as it was for the year in which he wrote it. The annual report of the Baptist Mission in China, issued in 1922, minced no words. 'It is perhaps safe to say,' concluded the Baptist missionaries, 'that today there is less of an organized government in China than there has been for a whole century.'

Such statements, however, had no effect upon the myth. Nor could the State Department afford to retract. Against the wishes of the other powers it had insisted on going ahead with the tariff conference and with the proposed reconsideration of extraterritoriality. But if, as MacMurray pointed out, the Chinese demands were met with respect to the tariff, the factional régime in Peking would be enriched without benefit to China as a whole. It was hardly possible for the United States to notify China publicly, however, that it had no government. Such a reversal 'would fail to be understood . . . and would meet quite likely with disfavour'.

While Mr Kellogg was explaining his dilemma to his minister in Peking, a full-scale civil war was again in progress in China. It began in Shanghai in May 1925, when the labour troubles which were chronic in the Japanese-owned textile mills were now accompanied by a riot and a confrontation with the British police of the International Settlement. The crowd of labourers and students showed its temper by its slogans: 'Abolish extraterritoriality, cancel all unequal treaties.' A general strike, a boycott which for more than a year transformed Hongkong from a prosperous port into a deserted town, cooperation between the Kuomintang and the Peking régime in levying demands on the diplomatic corps, major riots in Hankow and other cities of central and south China, showed this to be a bold uprising on a nation-wide scale more menacing to foreigners than the student-led May Fourth Movement. Even while the tariff conference was holding meetings in Peking in October 1925, the Forbidden City was under siege. Naturally the diplomatic corps recalled the dangers it had faced during the Boxer uprising; and MacMurray felt sure-footed in declaring China to be in a state of anarchy.

Meanwhile the Kuomintang in Canton had formed a connection with the Soviet Union whose capable representative, Mikhail Borodin, was teaching it how to become a revolutionary party of peasants and workers preparing for the conquest of China and the expulsion of the Western powers. By voluntarily repudiating the unequal treaties the Bolsheviks gained the friendship of Chinese nationalists. Chiang Kai-shek was dispatched to Moscow for additional training, and when he returned he was put in command of the newly-established Whampoa Military Academy; the Chinese Communist Party was merged with the Kuomintang; and Sun Yat-sen under Borodin's influence proclaimed his revolutionary Three Principles of the People. 'Whose semi-colony is China?' Sun demanded. 'China is the colony of every nation that has made treaties with her, and the treaty-making nations are her masters. China is not the colony of one nation but of all, and we are not the slaves of one country but of all.' The statement hardly brooked denial.

In May 1926 Chiang Kai-shek, having been made head of the party after Sun's death, embarked on the Northern Expedition intending ultimately to take Peking, and in five months made himself master of the Yangtze valley. The treaties were now waste paper wherever the Nationalists were in control, and mob attacks on the British concession in Hankow and on the International Settlement of Shanghai were inseparable from the aggressions of the Kuomintang. A general strike in Shanghai in March 1927 opened that city to Chiang Kai-shek, and almost immediately another serious outbreak

41, 42 The civil war in China. Chiang Kai-shek acclaimed on his arrival in Hankow, January 1927, and, right, Chinese men and women, charged with strike-breaking, before a tribunal of strikers at Canton, 1926.

occurred in Nanking, instigated, according to the American consul, by Kuomintang troops acting under orders. These troops, however, were apparently Communists who, in spite of the merger with the Kuomintang, had kept their identity as a party. Since the May 1925 incident the party had grown enormously in numbers and in strength, using the general strike to paralyse local government and attracting peasants by the thousands to its ranks. Apparently it was well on the way to making itself master of the Kuomintang.

Suddenly on 21 April 1927 Chiang Kai-shek double-crossed his Communist allies, descending on them in force in Shanghai and conducting a reign of terror that decimated their ranks and drove Mao Tse-tung and the remnants of his peasant army into exile in the mountains on the border of Hunan and Kiangsi provinces. This extraordinary purge enabled Chiang to make Nanking the Nationalist capital, and to advance the next year on Peking. At the time the northern capital was under the thumb of the Manchurian warlord, Chang Tso-lin, who also had the Japanese to reckon with. In June 1928 Chang met a mysterious death, and Chiang Kai-shek in turn found his way to Peking blocked by a Japanese force. Two other Kuomintang generals, however, advancing from different directions, entered Peking without resistance. China was now ostensibly united under the Nationalists; but the Communists had not been annihilated as planned, and they continued to attract peasants to their ranks and to wage guerrilla warfare against their enemies.

Sentiment against the treaties, traceable in large measure to the missionaries and to the Protestant Churches, had been building up in the United States. Historically, as we have seen, the missionaries saw eye to eye with the business interests. The treaties were not 'unequal',

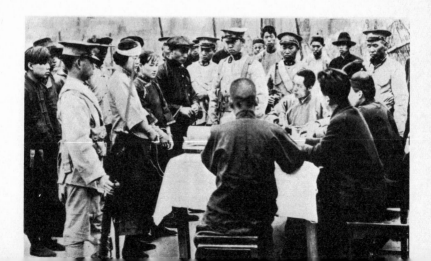

rather they were 'God's way of opening up the country to his servants'. But for the missionaries they had not worked out that way. Whether infected with communism or not, Chinese Nationalists attacked the missionaries as beneficiaries of the unequal treaties, as indeed they were; and with the outbreak of the civil war in 1925 the missionaries became as vocal as the Nationalists in denouncing the 'sinful' nature of the treaties. Extraterritoriality, declared the *Christian Century*, one of the most influential of the Protestant journals, 'is the perfect fruit of western imperialism in China', ripened at the cannon's mouth and enforced by gunboats and marines. With this change of heart the missionaries became the allies of the Nationalists, demanding an end to the unequal treaties without awaiting the outcome of the civil war. A resolution put through the US Congress in 1927 registered this feeling. To business interests and to career diplomats like MacMurray and Clarence E. Gauss, the consul general at Tientsin, the conversion was quixotic; to men like Tyler Dennett, who occupied a post in the Department of State, it seemed natural and timely. Dennett came from a missionary background and had written the important book *Americans in Eastern Asia*.[2]

A British Foreign Office memorandum, dating from December 1926, also favoured the Nationalists and professed readiness to deal with the Kuomintang on the basis of surrender of the treaty rights. The Foreign Office saw the Kuomintang as the ultimate victor, and by bargaining with the party in advance it hoped to break the ruinous boycott suffered by British business in the south. The memorandum embarrassed the American administration, to whom it was important to safeguard America's reputation as China's best friend; but in spite of these several pressures at home and abroad, the administration shrank from abandoning its theory that Peking was the central government of China. Only after the Nationalists had forced their way into Peking was this stalemate broken. A treaty granting Nationalist China tariff autonomy quickly followed in June 1928, and soon thereafter ten other treaty powers, Britain and Japan included, did likewise. Extraterritoriality, however, continued to stand until 1943.

Unity under the Nationalists was no more than superficial. Banditry and fighting were still China's 'most profitable business'. Civil war was the 'inexorable malady'. The consul-general in Shanghai reported on the warnings of T. V. Soong, the minister of finance, against the irresponsible military expenditures of the new régime. Although 'a very young man, scarcely thirty-five', Soong had an

43, 44 The civil war in China, 1927. A Communist soldier festooned with arms and utensils, and, right, a Nationalist soldier preparing to load a Stokes Mortar.

enviable record. 'Let us hope that he will be to China what Alexander Hamilton at the same age was recognized as being to the Federation of American States.' But a new oligarchy had been born at Nanking, a faction separate from the Kuomintang but calling itself 'the Government', an autocracy determined to perpetuate itself. Chiang Kai-shek was its leader, but Chiang faced a formidable rival in Marshal Feng Yu-hsiang. In the summer of 1929 there were six different armies under rival commands, and in October some twenty generals revolted against Chiang Kai-shek. China, thought the American chargé d'affaires, was heading back toward regionalism and decentralization.[3]

But Chiang, allied to Marshal Chang Hsueh-liang who ruled Manchuria from Mukden, had started a new adventure by seizing the Chinese Eastern Railway in North Manchuria and arresting some sixty of its Russian employees. Chiang, reported MacMurray from Peking where the American legation staff was still quartered, was carried away by the ease with which he had surprised the Soviets in their moment of weakness. The confiscation of the railway was part of his programme of whittling away at the treaty system, but the deed was done in 'the valour of ignorance', for the Soviets could not afford to be ousted from the railway. It was their single dependable link with Vladivostok, and they would be compelled to retaliate. Events soon proved that MacMurray was correct: before 1929 was over the railway was back in Russian hands. In the preceding February, the State Department learned from Tokyo of Japanese fears that the Nationalists would attempt a similar action against Japan's entrenched position in South Manchuria.

As China's nearest neighbour and largest customer, Japan had suffered more than any other power from lawlessness on the mainland. This was the judgment of the League of Nations' Commission of Enquiry, commonly known as the Lytton Commission, which was sent in 1932 to investigate the crisis which had arisen in Manchuria. During the 1920s Japan had intervened repeatedly to protect its nationals and their property in China, and the Chinese on their part viewed Japan as their major enemy. The American missionaries, having experienced their conversion against the treaties, took the same attitude: Japan was an incorrigible aggressor against China. But the Lytton Commission was historically minded. In its eyes the issue was not merely Sino-Japanese: it involved all the treaty powers, and as long as China was in ferment armed interventions were bound to occur. Till 1929 and later the American government adhered to a similar position.

Much like the great plains of the American West, Manchuria, when once pierced by railways, developed rapidly. Almost empty in 1896, it drew immigrants by the millions thereafter. From the congested provinces of Hopei and Shantung destitute Chinese farmers and labourers poured in, so that by 1930 the population totalled thirty million. Manchuria in short was a Chinese frontier, a far cry from the American 'new West' of Willard Straight's dreams. But Japanese capital and industry were indispensible to this development, as the Lytton Commission took care to emphasize.

The region was a tinderbox, however, a scene of cumulative and dangerous tensions becoming more taut after 1928, when Kuomintang propaganda bore down upon it. American consular reports from Dairen, Mukden and Harbin, available in Washington a full year before the Lytton Commission rendered its report, left no doubt on this score: 'Regarding Manchuria as her special field for capital investment and economic exploitation,' read one report, 'Japan has viewed with envy and concern the exclusive economic activity of the Chinese.' 'The Japanese had long been aggravated by Chinese *intransigence*,' said another. 'The Chinese would not – wilfully would not, from the Japanese point of view – come to a conclusion with the

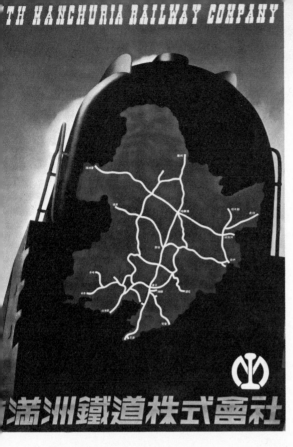

45 This poster of the Japanese South Manchurian Railway Company, 1931, shows a map of the railway system.

Japanese in negotiations over problems that affected legitimate Japanese economic development in Manchuria.'[4]

The Lytton Commission drew a concise but graphic picture of Kuomintang propaganda: its success in firing nationalist sentiment and in making life miserable for the small minority of Japanese who lived outside the Kwantung leased territory; its declared purpose of expelling the Japanese from Manchuria and of forcing surrender of the SMR. The Commission listed the numerous rights which Japan had acquired since 1905 and which centred on this trunk line. It directed attention to the competitive railway building and to the rate wars initiated by the Chinese in the hope of bankrupting the SMR. 'No railway of any importance has ever been constructed in Manchuria,' it remarked, 'without causing an interchange of notes between China and Japan or other interested foreign States.'

But the Commission went deeper than these rights and depicted the problem in terms of an irrepressible conflict. To the Chinese

121

Manchuria was an integral part of China, a region where the 'rights recovery' movement had special significance. Manchuria was a buffer, 'a region which constitutes an outpost against the penetration of Japanese and Russian influences. . . . The facility with which China, south of the Great Wall . . . can be invaded from Manchuria has been demonstrated to the Chinese from historical experience.'

Curiously, as the Commission realized, the Japanese mentality was similarly affected. 'The vision of a China, unified, strong and hostile, a nation of four hundred millions, dominant in Manchuria and in Eastern Asia,' observed the Commission, 'is disturbing to many Japanese.' Russia, however, was much more to be feared. So when Japan underscored its 'special position' in Manchuria, it was not referring merely 'to what is legally defined in treaties and agreements'. The Commission expressed the inner Japanese meaning as follows:

Feelings and historical association, which are the heritage of the Russo-Japanese War, and pride in the achievements of Japanese enterprise in Manchuria for the last quarter-century, are an indefinable but real part of the Japanese claim to a 'special position'. It is only natural, therefore, that the Japanese use of this expression in diplomatic language should be obscure, and that other States should have found it difficult, if not impossible, to recognize it by international instruments.[5]

An explosion of uncertain origin on the main line of the SMR just north of Mukden set afire this impending conflagration. The incident, trifling in itself, occurred at night on 18 September 1931; and the Japanese army, having a carefully prepared advance plan, put it into operation 'with swiftness and precision'. All its forces in Manchuria and some from Korea were brought into action almost simultaneously. The city of Mukden was occupied before the night was over, and then followed a series of campaigns which, in slightly over three months, cleared the entire country – a land as large as France and Germany combined – of Chinese troops. Except for bandit raids, the Chinese offered no resistance, partly owing to the continuing feuds with rival generals south of the Great Wall.

With the Japanese army carrying the war right up to the wall at Shan-hai-kuan in January 1932, Japan was the undisputed mistress of China's three eastern provinces. Even in the north, historically a Russian sphere of influence, the Japanese had their way. They occupied Harbin and Tsitsihar and made full use of the Russian-owned Chinese Eastern Railway. Soviet inaction, tantamount to an alliance with Japan, stands out in sharp contrast to the reprisal of 1929 against

46 The Japanese invasion of Manchuria. A Japanese officer and his men in the captured city of Shan-hai-kuan, February 1933.

the Chinese. Meanwhile, Chinese civil officials having fled, the Japanese proceeded with remarkable efficiency to develop new civil governments first in Mukden, the political capital of Manchuria, and then in the three separate provinces respectively. The Lytton Commission testified to the ease of these accomplishments and, while they met with acceptance on the part of the Chinese inhabitants, only Japanese troops and Japanese officials, both civil and military, made possible a new régime. The Commission investigated the systematic progress towards 'independence' which paralleled the military campaigns, and described at some length the government of Manchukuo, which was formally constituted on 1 March 1932.

American field officers in the Orient kept the State Department in Washington abreast of these developments. Aware of the resentments aroused in Japanese army circles at the execution by Chinese soldiers of one Captain Nakamura as a spy, the American minister in Peking had anticipated the coming of a serious crisis. It was settled policy on the part of the Chinese authorities to give the Japanese no satisfaction; and since the Kwantung army command was independent of orders from the war minister in Tokyo, it was capable of striking without warning and confident of its ability to rid the country of Chinese factions. Its swift success within less than four months demonstrated that it was right. From the American chargé d'affaires in Tokyo came the advice to keep clear. 'The situation presents so many anomalies that attempts to settle it by outside powers are likely to do more harm than good.' This was his recommendation soon after the trouble started.

Laurence E. Salisbury of the American embassy in Tokyo, with the help of the American consul-general at Harbin, conducted a field investigation in Manchuria which lasted nearly twenty days in October 1931, and wrote a report which was a masterpiece. Salisbury set forth the basic causes, described the systematic offensives of the Japanese army, made clear how opportune was the time chosen for action, and outlined the steps already being taken for the establishment of an independent administration in Manchuria. Salisbury was under no illusions that the Chinese inhabitants would be satisfied but he thought they would accept it. The Japanese, he reported, were making every effort to be conciliatory. This report, filed in Washington early in November 1931, anticipated the more detailed findings of the Lytton Commission by nearly a year. [6]

In the United States, and also in Western Europe, the crisis over Manchuria was featured as of outstanding importance. With the League of Nations functioning in Geneva, with the Nine Power Treaty of 1921 collectively guaranteeing the integrity of China, and with the Kellogg Peace Pact of 1929 renouncing war as 'an instrument of national policy', the world was aghast at the failure to halt the Japanese advance. The investigations both of the American field service and of the Lytton Commission, which arrived on the spot only to find itself confronted with a *fait accompli*, show Manchuria as a very knotty problem. Manchuria was notorious as a bandit centre, declared the Salisbury report, and the Japanese were determined to stamp this out and 'to see that Manchuria will be governed independently of the rest of China by Chinese who will be amenable to Japanese suggestion'. While critical of the extent to which Japan had gone in making a puppet out of Manchukuo, the Lytton Commission nevertheless recommended an autonomous régime barely different from that imposed by Japan. Declaring that Manchuria was without a parallel in other parts of the world, the Commission dismissed the notion that Japan had been guilty of a simple act of aggression.

The guilt thesis, however, persists to this day, the Japanese aggression being viewed as morally indefensible and the failure of the powers, acting through the League of Nations, to stop it being adjudged catastrophic. The League, trying by diplomacy to cope with the crisis, failed ignominiously, and the complete success of the Japanese military in attaining its end inaugurated a decade of international violence culminating in the outbreak of the Second World War. But, as has been shown, the problem was insoluble except by the means that Japan employed, and as a matter of fact no workable alternative was even suggested. The Council of the League, sitting in Geneva, tried to enlist the moral support of the American government, and a legend subsequently developed that the latter joined in and furnished the League with leadership. The Secretary of State, Henry L. Stimson, committed himself to print five years after by writing in his book, *The Far Eastern Crisis*, that he had created 'a new clear precedent of frank outspoken American co-operation with the League in a case affecting the general peace of the world'.

There is no doubt that the League Council wished to make a test case of this crisis and that it was hopeful of success if it got American co-operation. There is also no doubt that desultory conversation occurred regarding the application of economic sanctions as leverage upon Japan. Moral disapproval, however, was the sole factor that emerged from the intensive deliberations in Geneva and in Washington, not to mention London and other European capitals. Parenthetically let us note that the USSR, naturally best situated for intervention, was not involved and was still unrecognized by the United States.

The Official Journal of the League and some fifteen hundred pages of diplomatic documents published by the State Department in 1947-48 supply the authentic record. In summary it is as follows. First, Stimson, hopeful that the moderate elements in Japan would rise to the top, favoured a hands-off policy. Intercession by the League, even the dispatch of a commission of investigation, which the Council actually decided to do in September 1931, 'would do more harm than good . . . it would arouse all the national spirit of Japan behind their military people.' Second, he rejected the pleadings of his representatives in Geneva that they be authorized to sit with the League Council. If this were permitted, it 'would run into all of the other objections which exist in America about formal official action on the League'. In saying this the Secretary was simply recognizing the strong anti-League prejudice in the United States that had taken root

during the stormy debates over the peace treaty in 1919. Third, Stimson did realize the gravity of the situation even before he heard from his envoys in the Orient, and he wanted to 'leave a ladder by which Japan could climb down'. In acting rashly the Japanese had made 'a great mistake' – something that the Secretary personally regretted 'because I regarded Japan's welfare in her position on the outskirts of the Asiatic continent as very important to the Western world and I was sorry that she had put herself in a position which would probably in the long run end up by doing her serious harm.' On another occasion he drew an interesting analogy between Japan's problem in Manchuria and the 'situation that we have had to confront on the borders of Mexico and in Central America. Japan has undoubtedly suffered great aggravation in the past', although in making this attack she had exceeded the bounds of 'proper intervention'.

But, being resolved at all costs not to risk a war over Manchuria, the Secretary frankly stated, 'We do not care what solution is reached between China and Japan so long as it is done by pacific means.' To this President Hoover contributed his hope that a civil government could be set up in Manchuria under a viceroy mutually acceptable to China and Japan. Stimson, however, understood the extent of Sino-Japanese bitterness too well to believe this to be possible, and his minister to Peking, Nelson T. Johnson, reminded him of

47, 48 The Japanese invasion of Manchuria. Cartoons in *Punch* (1932, 1938) attacking the feeble British and American protests at Japan's action, left, and Japanese brutality towards the Chinese in Manchuria.

what he already knew: that China had no government capable of maintaining its sovereignty in Manchuria and that there was no alternative to the Japanese conquest.[7]

Over the transatlantic telephone Stimson held lengthy conversations with Charles G. Dawes, the American ambassador to Britain, and with Sir John Simon, the British Foreign Secretary. Should the United States align itself with the League, a step which Simon urged but which Stimson rejected, or should it try the Nine Power Treaty and the Kellogg Peace Pact on Japan? Meanwhile the Japanese completed their conquest of Manchuria; but Stimson, making it appear that he expected Japan to give up and somehow settle with China by 'peaceful means', published a note announcing that the United States would not recognize any situation brought about contrary to the Kellogg Peace Pact. This note of 7 January 1932 subsequently won fame as 'the Stimson doctrine', and on 23 February he took up the same theme in a lengthy letter to Senator William E. Borah. Both of these communications were obviously intended for public consumption. The letter held out the false hope that non-recognition would 'effectively bar the legality hereafter of any title or right sought to be obtained by pressure or treaty violation', and it vindicated the traditional American illusion that the United States was following the path of high principle independently of Europe and the League.

49 A Chinese poster, from Kiangsu province, demands the boycotting of Japanese goods, 1932. The Chinese people are shown ready to use an axe against the monster which has just bitten off the Three Eastern Provinces of Manchuria from China.

But this was not quite the case as the Secretary of State presented it to the British ambassador on the very next day. Nothing having been done to calm the Chinese, whom the American minister, Nelson Johnson, had reported as getting dangerously aroused, Stimson, in fear of another Boxer rebellion, had written his open letter to Borah to make the Chinese believe that the United States was still their friend. This was his 'chief impelling motive', he said. In May 1932 he was still saying privately that his policy was to be 'absolutely neutral between China and Japan'. But actually he had ventured out on treacherous ground, as W. Cameron Forbes, the American ambassador to Tokyo, was quick to tell him. Striving to appear disinterested the secretary had accomplished just the opposite. Moral disapproval had infuriated the Japanese. The effect of the letter to Borah was 'extremely injurious', bringing the situation in Japan 'nearly to the danger point' and resulting 'in a feeling of pressure being exerted upon the Japanese from the outside such as I had hoped could be avoided. . . . The Japanese officials and the Japanese public interpret the Secretary's letter as being distinctly provocative.[8]

The 'Stimson doctrine' made an equally bad impression on the American diplomatic and consular corps in China, while it was standing witness to the spreading chaos in that country. Fighting and a boycott had brought large Japanese army and navy forces into Shanghai. Suddenly deprived of the Manchurian customs revenue and unimpressed by American non-recognition of Manchukuo, the Nationalist government, reported Nelson Johnson, was 'at its wit's end'. Johnson, like the new American ambassador in Tokyo, Joseph

C. Grew, realized that Japan could not retire from Manchuria. It was like a prairie fire: 'The fire begins because the grass is dry, and as it spreads the fire dries the grass ahead of it, thus making possible the extension of the fire.' Guerrilla warfare in the north would draw Japan south of the Great Wall. 'Chinese and Japanese are in the current of events and are being carried on.' Johnson, Grew, and Major General Frank R. McCoy of the Lytton Commission, who conferred with the former and with the members of the consular corps, agreed that Japan might be forced into war with the United States. The heads of the Chinese Nationalist government were certain that this would be the end result, and they sent an envoy to Washington to try for an American commitment to supply China with arms. [9]

Thoroughly alarmed over the American do-nothing policy – for that was the central feature of the 'Stimson doctrine' – Johnson in September 1932 proposed an international conference to meet in Tokyo. The choice would mollify the Japanese and, on their home ground, it was possible that they would agree to cooperate in promoting an autonomous Chinese-Japanese régime in Manchuria. Historically Manchuria was autonomous and separate from China proper and, with this position firmly maintained, Japan might be made to feel reassured to the point of executing an honourable retreat. This was the recommendation which the Lytton Commission had agreed to make and which it had shared with the American and other concerned officials in China and Japan. The great merit of Johnson's proposal was that, if acted upon quickly, it would head off the fatal official Japanese recognition and military guarantee of Manchukuo that he knew was coming. 'Our position and interests in this area,' he cabled Stimson, 'demand that we do what we can to prevent the adoption by Japan of an Ishmaelite attitude towards us and the West.' [10]

Johnson's proposal was meant to implement the Lytton Commission's report, scheduled for publication in Geneva in October. But such bold statesmanship was too much for Secretary Stimson and President Hoover. On 15 September 1932, one week after Johnson's appeal, the Japanese government formally committed itself to the military régime in Manchukuo, thereby making the Lytton Commission's work a failure. But Stimson clung to his belief that all was for the best. The United States was in the right, and Japan would 'listen to reason'. So the 'Stimson doctrine' passed into history as one of the great triumphs of American diplomacy.

8 From friendship to enmity:
Japan and the United States, 1921-41

Outwardly the Washington Conference of 1921 restored relations between the United States and Japan to the firm foundation that had existed at the time of Theodore Roosevelt. Irritations that had approached the fisticuff stage during the quarrel over Shantung were smothered, fears of an arms race were dissolved, and mutual goodwill prevailed. Three treaties in particular emerged from this conference: the Nine Power Treaty guaranteeing the independence of China, the Naval Arms Limitation Treaty which put a stop to capital ship construction and established a fixed ratio in capital ship tonnage among the five principal sea powers of the world, and the Four Power Non-aggression Pact which provided for a demilitarized zone in the western Pacific Ocean. Locked together, these treaties constituted a seemingly perfect security system for the Pacific and Eastern Asia: none of the great powers could attack any of the others so long as it made no attempt to cross the neutralized zone.

Nevertheless there were basic weaknesses: treaties could not alter geography, which favoured Japan as the natural leader of the western Pacific; neither could they perform the miracle of raising up China, as it was pretended they could do, nor of erasing the developed sense of 'mission' held by the Japanese. China failed to improve, as we have already seen, although Japan during the ensuing decade disciplined itself under a policy of friendship and patience. This policy failing to yield results, the Japanese military in September 1931 repudiated it and speedily demonstrated the efficacy of its own methods. The new republic of Manchukuo was its handiwork.

In the meantime attitudes deeply rooted in the American tradition, which had caused hard feelings on previous occasions, again rose to the surface. Popular agitation and discriminatory legislation against the Japanese in the Pacific coast states reached the national level with the Immigration Act of 1924. California politicians, insisting that Japanese could not be assimilated by the white population and that they were objectionable on both racial and economic grounds, got an exclusion clause inserted into this act which in the case of European immigrants provided for a quota system.

Warning that exclusion would destroy the benefits of the Washington Conference, the Secretary of State, Charles Evans Hughes, tried to persuade Congress to omit the clause. Like the

Japanese ambassador to Washington, Mr Hanihara, Hughes was satisfied with Theodore Roosevelt's gentlemen's agreement; but the congressional committees on immigration twisted the argument by saying that the agreement had surrendered the sovereign right of regulating immigration into the United States to the Japanese government. Through the mouths of jealous nationalists like Hiram Johnson and Henry Cabot Lodge, the juridical and somewhat mystic concept of 'sovereignty' was lowered to the level of mass propaganda – it was invoked with equally telling effect to defeat the contemporaneous move to make the United States a member of the World Court. Thinking that a friendly letter which Mr Hughes could make public would help, Hanihara wrote to the Secretary of State. But neither the ambassador nor the Secretary anticipated the behaviour of Senator Lodge and his colleagues. By tearing one phrase – 'grave consequences' – out of context, Lodge converted Hanihara's letter into a 'veiled threat' against the United States; and in the face of further efforts, in which President Coolidge joined, to keep the exclusion clause out of the act, the bill passed by large majorities in both houses.

The other attitude, well-meaning but weighted with trouble in the 1930s, was formalized by the Kellogg Peace Pact of 1929. In signing this pact, which originated in American ideas of international morality, the fifty-two signatory states pledged themselves to 'renounce war as an instrument of national policy'. In popular terminology the treaty made war between or among nations a 'crime', but oddly enough American sentiment backed away from any proposals to devise a punishment that would 'fit the crime'. Like other nations, the United States kept its right to wage war in 'self-defence'. (Civil wars, such as the perennial struggle in China, were not 'crimes', however: they were 'domestic' affairs.) Moreover, as the Secretary of State made crystal clear, the United States incurred no obligation even to try enforcement measures, such as were stipulated in the Covenant of the League of Nations. The treaty had the force of a Sunday school pledge, no more and no less.

American opinion, official as well as popular, took this anti-war pact seriously, however. Piloted by William E. Borah, one of the bitterest critics of Japan during the Shantung crisis, it went through the Senate with almost a unanimous vote. Subsequently both President Hoover and Henry L. Stimson, who followed Kellogg at the State Department, made it the cornerstone of American foreign policy. Moral condemnation, it was presumed, would be sufficient to deter an 'aggressor', or induce him to desist from his aggression. Governments were expected as a matter of course to conform literally to the treaty. Otherwise they would stand condemned by the whole world.

The attitude was a perfect example of the 'devil theory of history', which persists in reducing a complex politico-social situation to a simple division between the innocent and the guilty. But like the ill-starred eighteenth amendment to the Federal Constitution, which prohibited the sale of intoxicating liquor, the Kellogg Pact was doomed to futility. American diplomacy devised the 'Stimson doctrine' as its means of enforcement; but far from shaming Japan it strengthened that country's passionate belief in itself so that, to modify slightly the text of Genesis 16:12, its 'hand will be against every man, and every man's hand against it'. The Japanese did indeed develop an Ishmaelite attitude, as we shall see.

Their first step, in February 1933, was to secede from the League of Nations. There was no bluff in their attitude, observed Ambassador Grew: 'The military themselves, and the public through military propaganda, are fully prepared to fight rather than to surrender to moral or other pressure from the West. The moral obloquy of the rest of the world at present serves only to strengthen not to modify their determination.' A Chinese appeal for financial help from Britain and America brought a warning in April 1934 from the Japanese foreign office, which regarded the appeal as a return to the familiar Chinese manœuvre of playing off one foreign power against another. Rumours of an international syndicate being formed in Paris and of foreign firms bargaining to sell aeroplanes and other accessories of warfare to China were disturbing. Borrowing the trite phrases inherited from John Hay's generation, the Japanese statement affirmed that Japan had a duty 'to exert the utmost effort in carrying out her mission and in fulfilling her special responsibilities in East Asia'. Differences in attitude toward China between Japan and foreign countries existed but could not be evaded, 'owing to Japan's position and mission'. That was why Japan had been 'compelled' to withdraw from the League.

Moderate elements in Japan, fearful of a premature war with Russia or America, were trying to keep the brakes on, reported Mr Grew; but despite some incompatibility between them, as represented by a 'cabinet of old men', and the younger generation, it was established national policy to win hegemony over East Asia. The ambassador was candid enough to recognize the affinity between this

50 The Japanese delegation, led by Y. Matsuoka (right), walking out from the Special Assembly of the League of Nations after the vote on the Committee of Nineteen's Report on the war in Manchuria had been taken, February 1933.

ambition and America's 'manifest destiny', but he was not optimistic: 'We shall sooner or later be seriously concerned as to whether the new generation will acquit itself successfully of the gigantic task to which the nation seems committed because American and Japanese policy in the Far East will directly conflict – unless,' he added, 'someone puts the helm over hard.'[1]

But no one either in Tokyo or Washington tried shifting the helm. American and British diplomatic officials watched the Japanese military and foreign office combine to put pressure on Nanking and on the provincial governors in North China. To demands for economic co-operation and political control the Chinese, lacking support from the West, were giving 'frightened acquiescence'. Economic co-operation meant following the pattern evolved in Manchukuo: ownership and management of the mines, railways, marketing of agricultural products, etc. by Japanese, exploitation of the abundant supply of cheap Chinese labour, China to be closed to Western enterprise and converted into a monopoly market for Japanese goods.

Political control meant that Japan would furnish the administrators in provincial and local government and send its own police to preserve order in China. By the summer of 1935 the five provinces of North China had submitted to Japanese rule, and in November they were formally detached from the Nationalist regime of Chiang Kai-shek. An 'atmosphere of gloom and fear' permeated Chinese official-dom. At any moment a minor Japanese officer might present his card and get whatever he demanded. 'I expect,' reported Nelson Johnson, 'to see Japanese activities, political and economic, increase in China from now on. . . . The Japanese Army is determined to break China to its will, whatever the consequences may be.'[2]

But Japan was not alone in threatening China with chaos. As a device for easing the depression in the United States and especially of appeasing the silver producing parts of the country such as Nevada, Congress enacted legislation raising the price the government would pay for silver. The law caused panic among the officials in Nanking, who realized that Chinese currency which was based on silver would lose all value once the United States, through its buying programme, started drawing the metal away from China. Appeals to the Roose-velt administration not to endanger China in this manner met with rebuff, but the Chinese averted fiscal disaster by a decree in November 1935 nationalizing the metal and prohibiting its export.

51, 52 The Chinese, both Communists and Nationalists, unite against their common enemy during the war against Japan. This machinegun, used by Communist Chinese soldiers of the Eighth Route Army against low-flying enemy aircraft, was captured from the Japanese. By contrast, the Chinese Nationalist officer, right, is equipped with German-made helmet, goggles, field-glasses, automatic pistol and motor-cycle.

In the meantime the Nationalists prosecuted their war on the Communists, undertaking five 'extermination campaigns' in the three years 1931-34. Chiang Kai-shek chose to make war on them rather than attempt a hopeless resistance against Japan. To escape their persecutors, who were pressing hard on them in Kiangsi province, some ninety to a hundred thousand Communists started on the Long March from Kiangsi in the south-east to the remote mountain fastnesses of Shensi in the north-west. A French writer compares this epic journey, from which less than eight thousand men survived, to Xenophon's Anabasis and to Napoleon's retreat from Russia. The Long March took a year, from October 1934 to October 1935: '10,000 kilometres, in the course of which the Communists crossed mighty rivers and soaring mountains, leaving behind thousands who died of exhaustion, cold, hunger, or thirst'.[3]

Both because America's attention was riveted upon Japan and because it was hostile to communism, which it identified with Moscow, it displayed slight interest in the Chinese Communists and their remarkable odyssey. Even the diplomatic corps in China showed comparative indifference, although the superior spirit and determination of the Communist soldiers, 'poorly equipped, underfed, and worn out from years of fighting', did not escape the observant eyes of some of the consuls. The contrast, as one declared, was 'but a pathetic commentary on the hopeless disorganization, petty rivalry, and general inefficiency' of the Nationalists. The Japanese, Nelson Johnson remarked sarcastically, would exploit the word 'communism', to justify their intervention, as they had exploited the word 'bandit' in the Manchurian campaign. 'It is a clever word to use because all the world now hates the communist who is associated in the newspaper public's mind with one who is against God, private property, and organized government.'[4] Chiang Kai-shek was still preoccupied with his 'bandit suppression campaign', however, and his ally from Manchuria, Marshal Chang Hsueh-liang, was supposedly engaged in harrying the Communists under that label in Shensi.

Meanwhile the American minister spoke of the improved spirit and desire for a united front against Japan which was emerging in 1936. Although apparently ignorant of the fraternization going on between Chang's men and the Communists in Shensi, Johnson knew of the latter's desire for an understanding with the Nationalists. Hatred of the Japanese furnished the common bond, and at least a faction in the Kuomintang shared this passion. Widespread student outbreaks vented resentment against the temporizing policies of Chiang Kai-shek. In June 1936 an insurrection of Kuomintang officers in Canton was an additional warning to Chiang to put more energy into his war on the Japanese than into the conflict with fellow Chinese. Obstinately, however, Chiang continued on his course: he would not accept the overtures the Japanese had been holding out to him, neither would he negotiate a truce with the Communist leaders who perceived they could never realize their ambition for a united front without the Kuomintang.

On 12 December 1936 a remarkable 'kidnapping' took place. In Sian, on the eastern edge of Shensi province, whither he had gone to take personal charge of the war on the Communists, Chiang suddenly found himself the prisoner of his own allies. The latter then summoned emissaries from both the Nationalist and the Communist headquarters in the hope of welding a united front. From Nanking came T. V. Soong and his sister Mayling, wife of Chiang; from Yenan, the Communist capital, came Chou En-lai. The sequel furnishes a perfect illustration of the maxim, 'politics makes strange bedfellows'. From being the 'watchdog of Japanese imperialism', the Communist view of Chiang Kai-shek in 1935, the Nationalist generalissimo became in little more than a year the 'living symbol of unity'. Even Moscow, which had been studying the situation, agreed

53 A scene in the reading-room of the workers' club, Yenan. Young people being shown portraits of Chinese and Soviet leaders, including Chu Teh (extreme left), Chiang Kai-shek, Sun Yat-sen, Stalin and Lenin.

that Chiang was necessary. In its anxiety to see Japan thwarted, the USSR accepted this unpalatable choice. With Russian backing a nominal united front was built up in China, which Moscow rewarded with a 'non-aggression pact' signed with Nanking in August 1937. By this time Japan had reopened the war, and from then until June 1941, when Nazi Germany invaded Russia from the west, Russia (or Germany through Russia) was the principal supplier of arms to the Chinese. The supply route led overland to Lanchow, the provincial capital of Kansu.

Meanwhile certain private interests in America and Britain, cheered by the signs of improvement in China and anxious to find a way out of the depression which had settled on both countries, relit the ancient faith in the China market. A privately financed American economic mission which visited the country in 1934 and talked to men like T. V. Soong returned the next year enthusiastic over the 'new China'. The Nationalists signified their wish for more railways, and Americans, British and even Germans rose to the bait. Schemes were hatched for lending more money to China, and discussions proceeded for reviving the international banking consortium. One of the foremost optimists was Sir Frederick Leith-Ross, sent out by the British Treasury to advise British businessmen in Shanghai. Sir

54 The American ship *Panay* sinking after being bombed by Japanese aircraft, 1937.

Frederick was sure that 'given a period of peace and good government China is going to be one of the biggest and best markets for our manufacturers'.[5]

Like the Cheshire cat, however, such dreams faded when an armed clash between Chinese and Japanese in a suburban area of Peking in July 1937 started a new and more enduring round of warfare. Panic set in among the Chinese in Shanghai, where the Japanese landed in August and began a great battle for possession of the Yangtze valley. By November Nanking was threatened, and Nelson Johnson moved his staff far up the river to Hankow. While standing by to evacuate the staff, the USS gunboat *Panay* was bombed and sunk by a Japanese aeroplane, on 12 December 1937, and HMS *Ladybird* and three Standard Oil tankers were likewise attacked.

The 'wild, runaway, half-insane men' (Secretary of State Hull's phrase) of the Japanese military were now on the loose. But far from stirring up war spirit in the United States, the attack, which was taken to be deliberate, enabled one of the leading pacifist congressmen, Louis Ludlow of Indiana, to attract serious public attention to his favourite panacea against war: an amendment to the Constitution stripping Congress of its power to declare war 'until confirmed by a majority of all votes cast thereon in a nationwide referendum'.[6] An expression of the prevailing 'keep out of war' spirit which had developed from the 1920s movement to outlaw war, the Ludlow amendment was voted down 188:209, a margin of only twenty-one votes. Pacifist complaints in the United States against Americans being permitted to remain in the Orient fitted in with demands of

Japanese military extremists that the West be ousted from China.

The real tragedy in the Orient, thought Nelson Johnson, was Japan. The struggle ramified 'into psychological, political and economic fields which are obscure . . . the Japanese military faction is forcing Japan along a road of compulsory piecemeal domination of China . . . nothing can save China from the necessity of deciding sooner or later whether to oppose Japanese aggression with force or sink to the condition of a vassal state'.[7] But it was China's problem, not America's, and Johnson, like Grew in Tokyo, advised against any form of involvement. There should be no mediation nor any attempt to bring about a truce.

In Washington the Roosevelt administration lived in fear of being 'pushed out in front' as leader of the League of Nations in a programme of economic sanctions, or of becoming 'a tail to the British kite', as Roosevelt himself informed Anthony Eden. But such phrases as 'bandit nations', 'arraigning Japan' before the bar of world opinion, invoking 'moral influence' in order to 'ostracize' that country, and especially of imposing a 'quarantine', nevertheless became part of American official jargon. These phrases emerged in connection with a striking speech by the President in Chicago in October 1937, about two months before the attack on the *Panay*. Pressed to define his idea of a quarantine, Roosevelt declared it to be 'a policy of isolation, severance of ordinary communications in a united manner by all the governments in the pact'. But sanctions, much less armed force 'against the unjust aggressor nation' were no part of his scheme; and, since Germany and Italy were also 'law breakers' and 'bandits', even attempts to 'ostracize' in the Greek sense seemed to lead nowhere.[8] The speech had sensational value, however, for it kindled hot discussion. Nervous lest sanctions be imposed, the Japanese met it with expressions of wrath. Most of the Chinese ports were by this time in their hands, and a month later Shanghai was theirs and the International Settlement at their mercy.

Understandably, with substantial interests at stake, the British wanted action but could do nothing without American co-operation. Only the United States could muster a sizable naval force in Far Eastern waters, if it meant business. But the Roosevelt administration was disinclined to make any boasts about the 'open door', much less even to suggest a programme of action. British proposals to summon a conference of the nine Washington treaty powers to meet in Washington were turned aside in favour of Brussels. The conference met in November, and the eighteen nations in attendance engaged in a futile debate about the need for a 'common attitude'. While the delegates were talking, the Japanese advanced on Shanghai and the Chinese prepared to transfer the seat of government from Nanking to Chungking deep in the interior.

Within less than a year Hankow and Canton were in Japanese hands, and in September 1939, five days after war had begun in Europe, Japan gave Britain and France 'friendly advice' to get out of China. Near to driving the civilian ministers in Tokyo out of office, the Japanese military had already made life unbearable for British subjects in Tientsin. They also came close to repeating the *Panay* incident by dropping bombs within two hundred yards of another American gunboat anchored in the Yangtze. Unwilling, however, to align itself with the British and French, the American government would go no further than verbalize its displeasure and ignore suggestions from Tokyo that a world conference be called to assure all nations of their 'proper places in the world'. Meaning was given to this phrase in November 1939 with the announcement that a puppet Chinese government would soon be established in Nanking and protected by Japanese forces with a view to 'combating communist activities'; and a year later Japan formally recognized this régime by treaty, making the elimination of communism the principal object of the two parties. Japanese attacks, however, had been mainly directed against Chiang Kai-shek in Chungking.

Emboldened by Hitler's humiliation of France, the Japanese foreign minister, Yosuke Matsuoka, became more specific on the meaning of Japan's 'proper place in the world'. 'The immediate aim of our foreign policy,' he declared, 'is to establish, in accordance with the lofty spirit of the *kodo* [imperial way], a great East Asian chain of common prosperity with the Japan-Manchukuo-China group as one of the links. We shall thus . . . pave the way toward the establishment of an equitable world peace . . . [and] in concert with those friendly Powers which are prepared to co-operate with us, we should strive . . . for the fulfilment of the ideal and the heaven-ordained mission of our country.' 9

Matsuoka could be quite poetic when he reached the subject of Japan's 'moral crusade' and its wish to see the world 'reorganized and reformed in a more rational way'; and, being aware of the current American effort to form a cluster of all the Latin American nations around the United States, he could argue for a 'regional understanding' of the countries of East Asia under Japan. In making Admiral Kichisaburo Nomura his ambassador to the United States,

55 The Japanese Foreign Minister, Y. Matsuoka, and the United States Ambassador to Japan, J. C. Grew, in conference in Tokyo, October 1940.

he chose wisely, for Nomura had the respect of his American naval colleagues and was known to be desirous of reconciliation between the two countries. But in the meantime, after needling the French through the summer, Matsuoka extracted an agreement opening Tonkin to Japanese military occupation and enabling the Japanese army to use the Indo-China railroad for an invasion of Yunnan province. The British in Burma were similarly isolated and coerced into closing the road temporarily from Lashio to Kunming. By these two steps Japan for the time being completed the encirclement of Chiang Kai-shek and hoped to force him into surrender.

Matsuoka's most sensational achievement, however, was his conclusion, 27 September 1940, of an alliance with Germany and Italy. The Japanese army command had advocated such an alliance even before the war in Europe started; and the Germans, especially after the 'destroyer-base' deal concluded earlier in the month between the United States and Britain, conceived of the alliance as creating a dangerous enemy who would distract American attention from the Atlantic. The Japanese anticipated, moreover, that this alliance would induce the Soviet Union to enter a non-aggression pact with them, protecting Manchukuo from a Russian attack and giving Japan a free hand against the Chinese Nationalists. Since Chiang Kai-shek was getting almost no support from the United States at this time, he too would have to succumb.

After paying their respects to the principle that 'every nation in the world shall receive the space to which it is entitled', with Germany and Italy to be the leaders in 'a new order in Europe' and

Japan to have the leadership in 'a new order in Greater East Asia', the parties arrived at the practical object of their alliance. They declared that they would 'further undertake to assist one another with all political, economic and military means if one of the three Contracting Powers is attacked by a Power at present not involved in the European War or in the Chinese-Japanese conflict'.[10]

On the face of it this text seemed to leave the United States in no doubt: it could not 'keep out of war' if it helped either Britain or China. Since America was already substantially aiding Britain, Joachim von Ribbentrop, the German foreign minister, wanted Japan committed if the Germans declared themselves 'attacked' in the Atlantic. But Matsuoka would not give Germany a blank cheque: what constituted an 'attack' by the United States, so it was secretly stipulated, could only be decided 'by a consultation among us three powers'. Mr Grew in Tokyo correctly guessed that this was the case. On the other hand, the Japanese armed services were about ready for their own moves: an invasion of southern Indo-China, Malaya and the Dutch East Indies, a surprise attack on Singapore and, most astonishing of all, a sudden mass attack on the American fleet at Pearl Harbor. Admiral Yamamoto conceived of the latter in January 1941: once the American fleet was destroyed, Japan need have no fears for its supremacy in the southwest Pacific. The American embassy in Tokyo heard that such a plan was afoot and passed the word on to Washington but, although the intelligence came from many sources, it failed to register with the Secretary of State. Nor was Mr Hull affected by the much greater possibility of a Japanese attack on Singapore. Such a move strongly tempted the Japanese navy, and von Ribbentrop tried to get Matsuoka's consent. When Matsuoka returned to Tokyo in March, armed with a neutrality treaty with Russia, he thought the way was clear for the southward advance. But a doubt remained. More clear-sighted than the State Department, the embassy in Tokyo in February 1941 warned the Japanese foreign office that an attack on Singapore would probably bring on a war with the United States. So Singapore and Pearl Harbor were linked together: if Japan was to establish the 'new order' for East Asia, it had to be freed of the danger of a flank attack from Hawaii.[11]

One other accomplishment was essential for the 'new order'. Since Chiang Kai-shek had rebuffed the repeated overtures made to him, he had to be eliminated. A non-aggression pact with the United States, it was thought, would speed this result. Chiang Kai-shek would be forced to yield, once American support was withheld.

Interminable conversations ensued between Admiral Nomura and Secretary Hull, Hull exhorting and Nomura listening to lectures on international law and justice. It seemed a basic premise with the State Department that Japan could not risk war with the United States and that therefore no compromise need be considered. To the Japanese this meant standing still while all the gains won since 1931 would be sacrificed.

Spurred by the German invasion of Russia, an imperial conference held in Tokyo on July 2 decided to plunge south: Japan would move into southern Indo-China, try to seal off the beleaguered Chinese régime in Chungking, hasten the plans for subjugating Malaya and the Dutch East Indies, and commence the necessary practice by sea and air for the raid on Pearl Harbor. Advance information of the Japanese intention to occupy Camranh bay and Saigon, the two ports in southern Indo-China, brought retaliatory action by the end of the month from the United States, Britain and the Netherlands: a total embargo on trade with Japan. Desultory talk about applying economic sanctions in order to bring Japan to book had been heard ever since 1932; the Roosevelt administration, through a system of licences affecting exports, had been making things gradually more difficult for the Japanese; but this action was so drastic as to compel Japan either to retreat or to risk all.

'The vicious circle of reprisals and counter reprisals' had begun, as Mr Grew expressed it. Most vital to the Japanese, of course, was the question how they were to get oil. In China too they also found themselves at a disadvantage: Russia's place as a supplier to Chiang Kai-shek was filled by the United States in the summer of 1941. An American military mission arrived in Chungking and a volunteer force, the Flying Tigers, began a war with Japan on China's behalf. If the Nationalist régime was to be rescued, the action came none too soon, for China, in the estimation of the American financial adviser to Chungking, was again on the verge of disintegration. The perennial problem of Chinese survival was still there: 'Back of all is the need for improvement of the administrative machinery of the Central, Local and Provincial Governments.' But the problem was 'extraordinarily difficult and complicated'.

Implicit in this whole matter was a basic difference of opinion between Ambassador Grew and his staff in Tokyo on the one hand and American officialdom in Washington on the other. Considering subsequent developments, the difference is of more than passing academic interest and so it should be stressed. Uninformed in advance

143

about the embargo imposed in July but well informed on the political realities in East Asia, the embassy was sure that Japan, if driven into a corner, would attack, but that in the long run it would lose. Hence it proposed to make every effort to meet the Japanese half way. With President Roosevelt personally Mr Grew raised the question 'whether it is in our own interest to see an impoverished Japan reduced to the position of a third-rate Power'. Mr Grew's evident lack of faith in Chiang Kai-shek's régime was supported by an eleventh-hour report from Clarence E. Gauss, the ambassador in Chungking who had had thirty-five years of experience in China. Chiang wanted the United States to crush Japan; he and his wife Mayling were 'unrestrainedly critical . . . [of] our failure precipitately to plunge our country into war . . . [and were] seeking to influence official American opinion through other than the regular diplomatic channels'. Because its hands were full with sustaining Britain in the Atlantic, the navy shared this distaste for a war in the Pacific.

Diametrically opposed to these views was the uncompromising Dr Stanley Hornbeck, adviser on political relations in the State Department and one-time disciple of Paul S. Reinsch of World War I days. Hornbeck was intellectually the *alter ego* of Cordell Hull and could always be relied upon to 'stand firm on our principles'. To him the crisis was solely of Japan's making and, he kept saying, that country was already 'half-beaten' and would not start a war with the United States. Therefore no concessions need be made. Hornbeck's confidence in his own infallibility is staggering: ten days before the Pearl Harbor attack he was ready to 'wager even money' there would be no war for at least three months. Admittedly more dogmatic than even Cordell Hull, Hornbeck was representative of the stiff hostility of the State Department toward Japan.

No better illustration of the gap between the embassy in Tokyo and the State Department in Washington can be found than in their respective attitudes toward a peace conference, the idea for which originated with Prince Konoye, the Japanese premier. Konoye first broached it in April, three months before the embargo. He wanted to meet President Roosevelt personally in Honolulu. Early in August, after the embargo, he renewed his proposal and softened his terms regarding Indo-China. Ambassador Grew snatched eagerly at the proposal, lauded Konoye for courage and statesmanship, analyzed the concessions he believed the Japanese would make, and declared his opinion that here was the chance for at least arresting the accelerating drive toward a head-on clash between the two countries. The throttling effect of the embargo was creating a psychology of desperation. Incalculable good might emerge from such a conference, and 'an utterly futile war' be averted. The alternative was the seizure of power by the military extremists in Tokyo, followed by an 'all-out do-or-die war'.

President Roosevelt favoured the idea, suggesting only that Juneau, Alaska be substituted for Honolulu as the meeting place. Cordell Hull, however, opposed it and in the end got his way. Preoccupied with matters relating to Britain, especially with his conference with Churchill in August from which Hull was conspicuously excluded, Roosevelt had left Japanese affairs largely to the State Department. It seems likely that Hull and his subordinates feared that the President, meeting with the Japanese prime minister face to face, would take matters out of their hands. Successful inroads on the State Department's prerogatives had previously been made, notably by the Secretary of the Treasury, Henry Morgenthau.

The argument against the proposed conference developed within the State Department can be summed up as follows. First, the embargo had not taken Japan by surprise (a direct denial of the evidence submitted by Mr Grew). Second, Grew's concept of an intense crisis was 'in considerable degree out of perspective'. The only real crisis was inside Japan, whose leaders must decide 'definitely and conclusively' between going on with their programme of conquest and returning to the four 'sound principles' which Hull had been trying to teach Nomura, viz.: territorial integrity and sovereignty of all nations, non-interference in the internal affairs of other countries, equality of all nations, and non-disturbance of the *status quo* in the Pacific. The Department's third point was that until the Japanese had subscribed to these principles and had stated in advance the terms they would offer, the proposed conference would be useless. Thus a wet blanket was thrown over Prince Konoye's offer, and late in September Roosevelt turned it down. To be sure, the State Department was not the only negative factor. Friends and supporters of Chiang Kai-shek in both Chungking and Washington also protested shrilly.

A last ditch drive for a compromise peace came from Tokyo in mid-November. Discouraged, Prince Konoye yielded the reins to General Hideki Tojo who, it was thought, could keep the army under control. Nomura in Washington was also discouraged, and upon his entreaty the Tojo cabinet dispatched Saburo Kurusu, an experienced diplomat, with proposals for an accommodation. Tired out by his long air journey, Kurusu reached Washington on the 17th with orders to conclude a settlement by the 25th, after which date 'things are automatically going to happen'. To be ready to spring if the moment arrived, Japan sent reinforcements to Indo-China and a task force to a vantage-point in the Caroline Islands for an attack on the Dutch East Indies. The sailing date for the Pearl Harbor expedition was set for the 25th.

But in the meantime it was hoped that Kurusu could arrive at a stand-still agreement with Washington: Japan to withdraw from southern Indo-China and confine itself to the north; the United States to restore normal commercial relations, including relief for the Japanese oil shortage; the United States also to allow Japan a free hand in making peace with China. Prodded by the armed services, which pleaded their unreadiness for hostilities in the Pacific, the State Department prepared to temporize with Japan for three months: it would agree to the military arrangement for Indo-China, stipulating that the number of Japanese troops be limited to 25,000, and it would partially lift the trade restrictions. But this offer was not even shown to the Japanese, Hull's explanation being that 'a bitter fight . . . would be projected by Chiang Kai-shek and carried forward by all the malcontents in the United States'. Considering the prejudices and the uncompromising attitudes of Hull and his associates shown repeatedly during the preceding years, the 'explanation' cannot be accepted on faith.

As a substitute for a temporary working agreement the Japanese received from the hands of the Secretary of State a document which Hull declared was 'a plan of a broad but simple settlement covering the entire Pacific area as one practical exemplification' of a permanent

56 This *Punch* cartoon of 1941, satirizing the Japanese apprehensive awakening to the American presence in East Asia, features Kurusu, the Japanese diplomat who went to the United States for talks shortly before the attack on Pearl Harbor.

57 Pearl Harbor, December 1941.

programme for peace. The 'broad but simple settlement' first enumerated Hull's cherished principles, and then outlined a series of steps in which Japan was expected to come down heavily on the American side with respect to China. The Japanese were required to withdraw *all* of their forces from both China and Indo-China and support *only* the régime of Chiang Kai-shek, giving up all their rights and concessions acquired since 1901. Even Manchuria was included in this sweeping call for surrender. But even if the Japanese had been willing to oblige, the document was impracticable on principle. Actually President Roosevelt himself contradicted it in a personal appeal to the Emperor of Japan. Roosevelt's message on 6 December ignored Chiang Kai-shek and spoke only of neutralizing Indo-China. But in the confusion and frayed tempers of the moment the message itself was ignored. The fateful raid on Pearl Harbor commenced at 8.25 the next morning.

9 The Chinese revolution stuns the United States

Fresh on the China scene in February 1942, General John A. Magruder, commissioned by the War Department in Washington to ascertain the military needs of the Nationalist government, soon took in the difference between the situation as he found it and the 'world of make-believe' which was the China of the American imagination. Fictitious symbols were preferred to cold facts, clever deception practised to convey a picture of China's prowess and of the 'marvellous achievements' of its army which were 'absolutely without foundation'. A great deal of 'alluring fiction' was being swallowed by the American public 'mainly because of Chinese propagandists . . . and because of the sponsorship accorded such propaganda on the part of many outstanding individuals, including missionaries as well as adherents to radical and liberal viewpoints. . . . [There was, for instance] the age-long practice of Chinese commanding officers of regarding their soldiers as static assets, to be conserved for assistance in fighting against their fellow-countrymen for economic and political supremacy.'

From its ambassador in Chungking, Clarence E. Gauss, the State Department was getting similar comments. Gauss, as we have seen, had thirty-five years of experience in China behind him, having served in various consular posts before succeeding Nelson Johnson at the embassy. China was 'only a minor asset [in the war], she might however become a major liability'. 'Chiang and the Chinese have been "built up" in the United States to a point where Americans have been made to believe that China has been "fighting" the Japanese for five years, and that the Generalissimo, a great leader, has been directing the energetic resistance of China to Japan and is a world hero. Looking the cold facts in the face one could only dismiss this report as "rot".' On the contrary, Chiang Kai-shek seems 'to have lost his direct and active interest in military affairs in recent years and to have acquired a touch of unreality derived from a somewhat grandiose or "ivory tower" conception of his and China's role in world affairs'. His demands for lend-lease supplies were insatiable, and as leverage upon the American government he kept brandishing the threat of a separate peace with Japan. Gauss brushed this off as pure bluff. 'Even the Communist leaders' knew it was, 'for they tell us that it is a bluff and we should "call" it.' (Chou En-lai

58 Communist Chinese cartoon, 1937. T. V. Soong, as a servant of royalty, carries *sycee*, the obsolete silver bullion of China, as he balances upon the American flag. Below, H. H. Kung, the Finance Minister, offers for sale a banknote bearing the image of Sun Yat-sen.

was at that time the Communist delegate resident in Chungking.) Chiang's wife Mayling was the real source of this bluff, Gauss concluded: it fitted her 'impatient and captious attitude', and it was just the sort of thing that she was 'capable of concocting'.[1]

T. V. Soong, Mayling's brother, was Chiang's foreign minister, but Soong resided *in Washington*. President Roosevelt, the officials in both the State and Treasury Departments, and even the Joint Chiefs of Staff listened to him willingly, and it seems probable that he was the fountainhead of the Nationalist propaganda against which both Gauss and Magruder warned. Indubitably Soong had intimate ties with numerous congressmen predisposed in his favour and with like-minded magazine and newspaper editors such as Henry R. Luce, the one-time 'Yale-in-China' missionary and the owner of *Life* magazine. A man of unlimited ambition, Soong may indeed have had the brains of an Alexander Hamilton, but hardly the scruples or the statesmanship.

From the pen of John Carter Vincent, counsellor of the American embassy, came a penetrating analysis of the Kuomintang, which controlled the government and of which Chiang Kai-shek was the undisputed leader. It was 'a congeries of conservative political cliques whose only common denominator and common objective'

149

was to remain in power. It was a 'sterile bureaucracy depending upon the monied interests and the military for its support'. Chiang held these factions together through personal influence and the political acumen in which he excelled. He was a super-warlord, as the French authority, Lucien Bianco, characterizes him. Two cliques in particular dominated the scene – the 'C-C' clique of the two brothers Chen, and the 'Whampoa cadets', the officers who had helped Chiang in his rise to power and whom he kept in command regardless of their demonstrated incapacity for leadership. To this congeries was funnelled the main stream of American arms and ammunition to be hoarded for use in the expected renewal of warfare with the Communists. Anti-communism, declared Mr. Vincent, was an obsession with these officers; war-lordism was not dead, and strong management would be required to keep it from reviving. In summary, concludes this report, 'all the trappings for state socialism along Nazi lines are present: a strong party control under the 'C-C' clique; an effective gestapo under Tai Li; and a military power and organization, headed by Ho Ying-chin, thoroughly asocial in its outlook and bent on maintenance of its position and prerogatives in the national life'.

To borrow the expressive language of Lucien Bianco, China was (and is) 'a society of poor people in which even the well-to-do had very little property'. A 'rich' Chinese landowner could not stand comparison with his European, much less his American counterpart. Rarely could he claim possession of even fifty acres. It was a case of 'the very poor and the less poor'. For the country as a whole the average peasant family holding was 3.3 acres in the 1930s, but the population pressure on the land kept up relentlessly. On the great plain of North China it reached a 'density unknown in any other semi-arid region of the world'. In 1851 the total population was estimated at 432 million, in 1953 at 580 million, in 1970 at somewhere between 750 and 800 million. Obviously war and revolution were no checks on population growth. Neither were the natural checks of flood, famine and epidemic, pointed out by an eighteenth-century Chinese thinker, Hung Liang-chi. Hung's reasoning parallels that of the great T. R. Malthus, his English contemporary. 'The population within a hundred years or so can increase from five-fold to twenty-fold,' wrote Hung in 1793, 'while the means of subsistence, due to the limitation of the land-area, can increase only from three to five times. . . . The larger the population, the cheaper labour will be . . . the harder it will be for the people to secure a livelihood.'[2]

59 Chinese soldiers of the Eighth Route Army marching on the Great Wall during the war against Japan, 1938.

The reluctance of the impoverished peasantry to follow the Kuomintang widened and deepened the gulf between it and the Chinese Communists. The United Front erected at Sian in 1936 quickly turned into a false front. One can only marvel at the forbearance of Chou En-lai and his associates in freeing their prisoner, Chiang Kai-shek; and one must assume that their ruling motive was to forestall a possible deal between him and the Japanese who were hoping to induce him to serve their interests. But Chiang in his dreams of making himself the master of all China would make no deal with the Japanese, neither would he collaborate with his Communist rivals. Each régime maintained itself in its own territory, the 'Central Government' centred on Chungking and endeavouring to shield its domain against Communist infiltration, the Communists on their part holding the north-west provinces, Shensi, Kansu and Ningshia. Japan managed to occupy the seaports and the coastal

60, 61 China's gods dese-
crated. Japanese soldiers
in a shrine in Shensi, and
right, Communist Chinese
working at a printing press
in a temple, with a statue of
Buddha in the background.

fringe, stabilizing the front during World War Two along the
Peking-Hankow-Canton axis but, like Napoleon in Russia, baffled
by the vastness of the country and unable to conquer it. Meanwhile
hostilities between the two Chinese parties broke into the open as
early as the spring of 1938 and reached a climax in January 1941,
when a Nationalist army surrounded and destroyed the Communist
New Fourth Army in Anhwei province just south of the Yangtze.
Because of its energetic campaigns against the Japanese, the New
Fourth had gained popular favour, and its defeat at the hands of other
Chinese made its soldiers martyrs in the cause of Chinese nationalism.
Henceforward the real nationalists in China in the eyes of the peasant
masses were the Communists.

Not really aroused until after the Japanese invasion of 1937, the
poor peasants were the real revolutionaries and the Red Army was,
for a variety of reasons, a loyal peasant army in contrast to the badly

treated and badly led conscript army of the Kuomintang. As a class, the peasantry had 'a more distinguished tradition of struggle than any Western proletariat', and sinified Marxism 'proved itself the most effective system (the most effective "ism") not only for attacking social iniquities, but also for restoring a national pride that had been sorely tried for a century. *Here was a doctrine borrowed from the West that condemned the West.*'[3]

Wherever the Red Army took over, whether from the Japanese or from the Kuomintang, it took pains with the villagers, lowering rents for the tenants and taxes for the small landowners but not otherwise disturbing the social structure. Notable among its successes was the establishment of guerrilla units inside enemy lines and, imperilled by both the Japanese and the Kuomintang, young peasants chose to throw in their lot with the guerrillas. A border region government co-ordinated these various base areas, of which there

62, 63 Two Communist Chinese woodcuts: left, Communist Chinese soldiers attacking; right, the Communists reduce the rent on land for the peasants.

were nineteen behind the Japanese lines in 1945; and from its precarious hold on remote Shensi province in 1937 the Chinese Communist Party extended its rule over the whole of the North China plain into Shantung province. With Japan defeated and forced to evacuate, the Chinese Communists were more than half-way along the road to victory over the Kuomintang.

Expelled from Nanking by the Japanese and forced to establish its capital in the uncongenial setting of a rural market town, the Kuomintang (which was at one and the same time 'the Government') found itself far removed from the business classes of the seaports who were its natural supporters. Such few 'improvements' for which it could claim credit – railways and cross-country highways linking up the larger cities – benefited commerce but not the peasantry. 'Land to the cultivator' might still be a party slogan, but after a few feeble gestures earlier in their career the Nationalists made no attempt to compete with the Communists. The criticisms levelled at the régime by the American foreign service staff in 1942 had been valid for some years: the Kuomintang was the private domain of a few families, notably the Soongs and the Kungs, and its methods of keeping itself in power were indistinguishable from those of the decadent Ch'ing dynasty under the Empress Dowager. Like the Empress, Chiang Kai-shek kept his footing by playing off one side against the other and in his person he embodied the Central Government. In his single-minded pursuit of power he had the capable help of his wife Mayling; through the incorporation of four state banks and the manipulation of the currency and of loans supplied by the United States, this small inner group in control of the purse-strings managed to keep up the appearances of a sovereign independent state. Monies that did not go into the pockets of officials were diverted to the support of a large army, so that, to the unsuspecting, Nationalist China during the Second World War played the role of a 'great power' defending itself against its mortal enemy, Japan.

Among the unsuspecting none were so naïve and so unwilling to face these truths as were government circles in Washington. The 'experts' in the State Department disputed the reports of Magruder and Gauss. Chiang Kai-shek, they insisted, had a 'broad-gauge outlook'. He was a 'great leader' representing a mass movement, and through him 'China can constitute a valued and effective ally in the common war effort'. For four and a half years Chiang had 'successfully' fought the Japanese, and only Russia and America had given him any help. The writers of these memoranda recognized that China was imbued with 'a real spirit of nationalism', but they did not know who were the true nationalists. 'I never faltered in my belief,' declared Cordell Hull later, 'that we should do everything in our power to assist China to become strong and stable. It was obvious to me that Japan would disappear as a great Oriental power . . . the only major strictly Oriental power would be China.'[4]

The Military Intelligence Division of the War Department was much better informed, but its reports left no mark on the Secretary, Henry L. Stimson, who had but one thought – how to bring down Japan. The Communist army, concluded these observers, was 'considered the benefactor and saviour of the people not only against the Japanese, but also against the rule of landlords and the former warlords who had held supreme sway. . . . It is not the ideology of Communism as such that impresses the people. It is the practical results of Communist leadership'.[5]

Nothing better illustrates the blind zeal of the State Department, seconded by the Treasury Department, than its response to the demands of Chiang Kai-shek for a thousand million dollar loan, half of it to come from the United Kingdom (itself heavily dependent upon the United States), the other half from the United States. Chiang expressly declined to say how the loan would be used, but the American government gave him $500 million without attaching any conditions. (The United Kingdom forthrightly refused.) Presumably the loan would help bolster the Chinese currency, but as early as June 1942 Ambassador Gauss could write an 'I told you so' dispatch. Hoarding and speculation continued unchecked. Landlords and bankers were influential at Chungking, 'with the result that measures against their interests are in large degree opposed or made ineffective'. The Secretary of the Treasury, Henry Morgenthau, who allowed himself to be won over to the loan in the first instance, confessed failure to the President in December 1943. The loan had had 'little effect except to give additional profits to insiders, speculators and hoarders.' [6] But the lesson remained unlearned. Chiang was already demanding another thousand million on pain of economic and military collapse, and Roosevelt was committed over the heads of Churchill and Stalin to making China one of the postwar world's 'four policemen' responsible for keeping Japan down and Russia in proper restraint.

To the eyes of the embassy and its conscientious staff in Chungking this stage picture drawn by Roosevelt remained invisible. All through the year 1943, while the President was busy with the cause of China under Chiang Kai-shek, the embassy continued its investigations and kept Washington well informed of the multitudinous signs of breakdown and *de facto* civil war seen by its field officers on their travels through the interior. Disaffection in Szechuan, banditry in Kansu, a famine in Honan worse than any experienced within fifty years, another famine in south-eastern Kwangtung, scattered revolts in other provinces under the nominal control of the central government, bitterness toward the Kuomintang and resentment toward Chiang Kai-shek – these and other warnings were recurrent themes in reports from the field. Inflation was eating the heart out of China, guerrilla activity against the Japanese was non-existent. 'In the occupied areas the Japanese with a few hundred troops are able to sit behind their elaborate fortifications and contain thousands if not hundreds of thousands of idle Chinese troops.'

'I do not wish to go on record,' wrote one comparatively reticent official, 'as predicting that the Chiang Kai-shek régime will collapse tomorrow; it will probably be able to carry on for some time yet barring a widespread famine. But I do feel that the seeds of disintegration have been planted.' In May appeared the Kuomintang's new 'bible' – the book *China's Destiny*, written by Chiang himself. The book was a chauvinist tract putting the blame for all of China's ills upon the 'unequal treaties', but it stirred the anger of Chinese intellectuals. They resented Chiang's attempt to set himself up as a 'Sage' as well as a 'Hero', invading a field for which his background and intellectual attainments had not equipped him. Chiang had a

64 Chou En-lai.

reputation for political acumen and skill in manipulating people, but he did not command the loyalty of his troops, apart from the secret police. The latter maintained 'thought correction camps' near Chungking, reported Mr Gauss, and the victims were kept in caves and if ever released were 'usually broken both in body and in mind'.

Meanwhile Chou En-lai, remaining in Chungking as Communist representative until the middle of the year, talked freely with the embassy staff, whose respect he earned, and urged that American officers be stationed as observers in Shensi and Shansi, the Communist-held provinces. This was a move which Major-General Stilwell, assigned by Roosevelt to open a route through Burma into China, heartily advocated when informed of the superior fighting qualities of the Communists. Chou did not agree that China needed massive American succour and, wrote the American chargé d'affaires, 'he deplores the present virtual military inactivity in China and speaks regretfully and reproachfully of the lack of offensive spirit shown by the Kuomintang leaders'. When in September Ambassador Gauss returned to Chungking from a futile errand to Washington, he verified the repeated warnings of his assistants of the coming civil war and commented on the unreasonable demands of Chiang Kai-shek that the Communists disperse their army and place themselves at his mercy.[7]

These carefully prepared factual reports rendered by the American foreign service and published long after when Chiang Kai-shek, a refugee on the island of Taiwan, was still masquerading as the leader of 'Free China', are a classic study in diplomatic frustration. In Washington they received only perfunctory attention, indeed it is possible they were not even read: only occasional reactions on the part of the subordinates in the lower ranks are recorded, and, since they were so at variance with the crusade to make a 'great power' out of China, they were assuredly not destined for a receptive audience among the makers of policy. A personal interview between the President and the ambassador was equally barren. A 'rank amateur' in diplomacy as well as in military matters, and subject to 'whims, fancy and sudden childish notions' (Stilwell's unvarnished opinion), Roosevelt was condescending toward professionals.

Roosevelt dwelt in the Chinese 'world of make-believe', and Chiang Kai-shek was the hero pictured as 'fighting' Japan for five long years. 'We must have China to get at Japan': this was an American imperative as strong with the professional military as with the President himself. But to 'have' China was not easy, the sole approach being though India and Burma. T. V. Soong proposed the perilous and costly air route over the Himalayas to Kunming, where supposedly the lend-lease equipment and supplies would be put in the hands of Chiang's generals who would then push the Japanese into the sea. This scheme was taken up with great zest by General Claire L. Chennault, who saw himself as leader of the American volunteer Flying Tigers forcing Japan into quick surrender. Five hundred planes would accomplish this feat, and the war would be over in 1943. Not only Roosevelt but several of his cabinet officers too shared this enthusiasm.

From the Chinese came a second proposal which was adopted with equal doggedness and prosecuted with equal extravagance, only to terminate in tragic failure in 1944. This was the famous Burma Road, immortalized by the great General Stilwell – 'Vinegar Joe', whose salty comments on Roosevelt, Chiang Kai-shek ('the Peanut'), Madame Chiang and many others were matched by his exceptional courage, honesty and understanding of practical military matters. At first Stilwell had scant faith in the project, and the contrast between his rugged honesty and the false picture drawn of his imaginary victory in 1942 comes into relief with the loss of Burma to the Japanese. A Chinese communiqué reported that the invader had been 'wiped out', and American newspaper editors at home swallowed the story whole; but Stilwell, escaping on foot across the mountains into Assam, gave a different version: 'I claim we got a hell of a beating. We got run out of Burma and it is humiliating as hell. I think we ought to find out what caused it, go back and retake it.'[8] Against overwhelming odds the recovery of Burma and the construction of a road across the high mountains and steep ravines of the interior became Stilwell's great passion. Hopefully the road would lead to Kunming and be the instrument for making a 'great power' out of China.

Stilwell, however, soon learned that Chiang Kai-shek was really 'waiting out the war', confident that the United States would win it for him but always with his hand out for more supplies. 'The Generalissimo is probably the only Chinese who shares the popular American misconception that Chiang Kai-shek is China,' drily remarked John P. Davies, sent by the embassy to serve as Stilwell's political adviser. Davies appreciated the contrast between Kuomintang corruption and Chinese Communist proficiency, and he pressed for a direct political and military liaison with the latter. Enraged by Chiang's 'skullduggery and double-crossing' and himself bitterly disappointed by the diversion of supplies to the Atlantic theatres of war, Stilwell came to this view too. 'Peanut and I are on a raft,' he picturesquely wrote to his wife on Thanksgiving Day 1943, 'with one sandwich between us, and the rescue ship is heading away from the scene.' Despite his many frustrations, the doughty commander continued in the faith that China was indispensable. Properly supported from home and reinforced with fresh Chinese Communist troops under his command, he could wage offensive warfare and drive the Japanese from the mainland of Asia.

Chiang, however, was adamant. He hated Stilwell, a disobedient and recalcitrant general whose dismissal he now demanded of Roosevelt; and he would allow Communist troops only if they took orders directly from him. The generalissimo wanted another blank cheque, but this time (September 1944) he got from Roosevelt 'a crippled ultimatum' (Barbara Tuchman's neat phrase): Chiang must give Stilwell 'unrestricted command' of all Chinese forces, but should he refuse he need not worry. Washington would continue writing cheques for him anyway.

A crisis had come, but unfortunately the American government allowed the weak Chinese Nationalist régime to call its bluff. 'If you sustain Stilwell . . . you will lose Chiang Kai-shek and possibly you will lose China with him.'[9] Such was the word of the politician, Patrick J. Hurley, whom Roosevelt, paying no attention whatsoever to Ambassador Gauss, had sent to pacify Chiang. Hurley wore a major-general's uniform, but the Chinese caught on to him. They dubbed him 'the big wind'.

So both Stilwell and Gauss were put to the sacrifice, victims of the illusory optimism over Kuomintang China and the concomitant fear of communism. Ironically, however, the United States itself disproved its own thesis: with the advance of the navy in its 'island-hopping' offensive against Japan, attention shifted to the sea; and with the departure of General Stilwell the China–Burma–India theatre, on which untold blood and treasure had been lavished, diminished into a backwater. As the fatal day for dropping atomic bombs on Japan approached, China was temporarily forgotten.

Not Russia, however. Bent on invading Japan and punishing that country for its past sins, but at the same time fearful of the awful casualties expected to be inflicted on the American armed forces for exacting full retribution from the Japanese, the United States bargained eagerly for Soviet participation. At the Yalta conference (February 1945) Roosevelt and his subordinates believed they had made a friend and supporter of Josef Stalin. 'This was the dawn of the new day we had all been praying for,' recorded Harry Hopkins, Roosevelt's intimate adviser. 'The Russians had proved that they could be reasonable and farseeing.' Stalin had agreed to go to war with Japan 'in two or three months after Germany has surrendered'. To Russia in return would go all of its pre-1904 rights 'violated by the treacherous attack of Japan' in that year. Among these would be its 'pre-eminent interests' in the port of Dairen and the two railways, the Chinese Eastern and the South Manchurian, and the restoration of the original lease of Port Arthur as a naval base. Lip service was paid to the 'open door' and 'the sovereignty of China', and the Americans really believed it.[10] They seemed not to realize that Manchuria was Russia's any time it chose to invade; by its very nature the bargain was bound to be one-sided.

Stalin waited for the right moment. It came on the seventh of August, one week before Japan yielded to the United States. Atomic warfare having laid waste two of their cities, the Japanese opened their doors to a bloodless American occupation, while in Manchuria they resigned themselves to surrender to the advancing Russians.

'We ought to get out – *now*.' Blunt as ever, Stilwell so expressed himself as he watched the persistent folly of American interference in Chinese affairs. No matrimonial knot was ever so tight as the bond between the American government and its Chinese client, appointed to receive the Japanese surrender on the mainland but unable to reach the scene in North China and Manchuria unless brought there by United States transports. Three Nationalist armies – as many as five hundred thousand men, armed with brand new equipment – were carried by air and by sea from south of the Yangtze to vital coastal positions in the north. Fifty thousand US marines came to their aid in Peking, Tientsin, the adjacent coal mines and other areas. But when the transports arrived off Chefoo on the north coast of Shantung and at the Manchurian ports opposite, they were warned away. Chinese Communists occupied Chefoo – from their mountain stronghold, as we have seen, they had spread eastward across the North China plain into Shantung. With the Americans succouring the Nationalists, the Soviets threw their support to the Communists.

Theoretically both the United States and the Soviet Union were supposed to be neutral in the Chinese civil war, but the Americans rebuffed Communist complaints against their one-sided intervention while summoning the highly successful Communist General Chu Teh to take orders from the corrupt government at Chungking. The Soviets on their part capitalized their advantages in Manchuria, dismantling Japanese factories and taking whatever movable property they could commandeer as war booty. They barred the Manchurian ports to the Nationalists while thus plundering the country, but stood aside while Communist guerrillas infiltrated from North China. Joined by Japanese-trained soldiers of the former Manchukuo army and seizing Japanese arms and ammunition left by the Soviets, who confined their occupation to Dairen and the former leased territory, the Chinese communists got a head start. After finally locating a port outside Manchuria where they could disembark, a Nationalist army belatedly trudged across the border, and against the advice of his American protectors Chiang Kai-shek insisted on penetrating deep into the interior. The Communists allowed him easy victories in taking Mukden and Changchun, deceiving him into thinking that all of Manchuria would soon be his. But, in the words of the US White Paper, the splendidly equipped but incompetent Nationalist army 'at the end of a 1,000 mile-long supply line committed itself to a scale of operations it could not support, and opened the way to the eventual piecemeal destruction by the Communists of its widely scattered military units'.[11]

Meanwhile the ebullient Hurley, back in Washington, finally shed his illusions that single-handed he had won a pledge of support from Stalin in Moscow and a promise from Mao Tse-tung in Yenan for the pet American scheme of a 'coalition government' for China. Diplomatic officials, from Averell Harriman in Moscow to Davies and Service in Chungking, had been saying contrariwise, but Hurley in his self-conceit lacked their integrity. Forced by events to admit failure, he went to the newspapers in November 1945 with a wordy letter of resignation complaining that the professional diplomats had stabbed him in the back. They had plotted with the Communist Party and 'the imperialist bloc of nations' to enthrone the former in China. A 'weak American Foreign Service' was the enemy of American 'democracy and free enterprise'. Career diplomats are traditionally unacceptable to the American democracy, and Hurley's accusations, buttressed by enough half truths to make them sound genuine, found their mark. Agents and supporters of Chiang Kai-shek – the China lobby, whose fiscal agent was a New York importer and whose friends and advocates were legion in number among church groups, newspaper and magazine editors, and congressmen ready to make political capital out of the post-war disappointments – started a witch hunt with 'Communism' as their rallying cry.[12]

The United States was all along 'allied to a corpse', as one American general recognized, but the bewildered government in Washington continued to act in the belief that it could raise the dead. It was told by its new commander in the field, General Albert C. Wedemeyer, that China needed a guardian. The guardian, meaning the United States, might act in the name of the United Nations, but it should send its own forces to thwart the Soviet Union and the Chinese Communists. The 'presently corrupt, reactionary and inefficient' Nationalist régime could not be expected to behave responsibly. Yet this same régime, hated by the Chinese populace as Wedemeyer admitted, would bring peace and unity to China.

Recoiling from assuming an outright guardianship, the new American President, Harry S. Truman, decided on another try. Truman persuaded General George C. Marshall, a man of real stature, to make the attempt. Marshall sojourned in China for the whole of 1946, while the Kuomintang and its mortal enemy acted

65 Mao Tse-tung in
1938.

out their 'comedy of peaceful intentions', to borrow an expressive
French phrase. Mao Tse-tung and Chou En-lai even obliged Marshall
with a prolonged visit to Chungking, but the American envoy failed
to impress Chiang Kai-shek. Marshall had the example of French
Communists joining a coalition party government in Paris in that
year, but the Chinese civil war was too much of a reality to profit
from the French example. The war went on in Manchuria, the
Russians evacuating, and the Chinese Communists, by a series of
masterly retreats, allowing the Nationalists to deceive themselves
that they were winning. By keeping up the flow of supplies to the
latter the American government undercut its own envoy. Marshall
left the country in January 1947, his mission a total failure.

66 Madame Chiang.

Under 'the world's worst leadership' the Nationalists during the next two years stumbled from defeat to defeat. By contrast the Communist leaders were 'men of proven ability who invariably out-general the Nationalist commanders'. This comparison was made by Major-General David Barr, and the story of the Nationalist *dénouement* is told in matter-of-fact style in the US White Paper. Barr headed another advisory group sent over in the fond hope of re-straining Chiang Kai-shek. In midsummer 1947 the Communists seized the initiative in Manchuria and kept it until, in October 1949, they captured the southern city of Canton and forced the Nationalist remnant to flee under American protection to the island of Taiwan. The White Paper narrates the master-strategy of the Communists, their high morale in routing Nationalist armies superior in number and better armed, the desertion of whole divisions from Nationalist ranks, the capture of city after city and the swift advance south of the Yangtze after the decisive battle of Hwai-hai, Chiang Kai-shek's Waterloo on a barren plain north of Nanking in November 1948. 'Nationalist China ended in chaos and apocalypse', to quote Lucien Bianco's terse conclusion.[13]

In spite of these mounting disasters, however, American diplomacy proved incapable of readjusting, and the United States continued to pour aid into the lost cause of Chiang Kai-shek. From the ambassador

67 Chiang Kai-shek.

in Nanking, a former president of a missionary supported university in Yenching, came a steady stream of reports throughout 1948 commenting on Kuomintang corruption, on Chiang's dubious favourites, and on the rising tide of popular hatred of the United States for perpetuating the civil war. But still the ambassador could not bring himself to give up Chiang Kai-shek – 'the only moral force capable of action', 'a strong, resourceful man unquestionably sincere and courageous', though the ambassador's own testimony did not justify such sentiments. Chiang was the missionaries' darling. Touching stories of his Christian piety had made him so; and according to *Time* magazine, owned by the son of a missionary, he and Mayling were the ideal married couple.

The supreme moment of irony arrived in March 1948 with the passage through Congress of the China Aid Act. Repeating the familiar creed of 'the genuine independence and the administrative integrity of China', which it identified with the cause of Chiang Kai-shek, and reaffirming its faith in Chiang's policy of 'self-help and co-operation', the act gave him another four hundred million dollars. The next month the victorious Communists captured Nanking and Shanghai and started on the final campaign of the revolution.

Missionary fidelity to Chiang made its weight felt through party politics in the United States, and the China Aid Act was the price exacted by Republicans in Congress in exchange for their support of the Truman administration's proposals for European recovery. Partisanship in the heated presidential election year 1948 brought moderate Republicans to the side of the passionate right-wing group who formed the hard core of the China lobby. If Communism won in China, it would win the rest of Asia and Europe too. 'Misguided liberals' and the 'Red cell' inside the State Department were lumped alongside the Chinese Communists as tools of the Kremlin; and regardless of the cost the United States should throw itself into China on the side of the Kuomintang. The Republican nominee, Governor Dewey, implied that if elected he would give unlimited assistance to the Nationalists; and the prestigious General Douglas MacArthur made known his willingness to head the crusade. Moving from the ridiculous to the absurd, MacArthur put in a word for the 'yet untapped opportunities for trade . . . in the advance of Asiatic races'.[14] Encouraged by such nonsense, the beaten Chiang appealed to 'the American people and their statesmen' to dedicate themselves afresh to the salvation of Asia; and Madame Chiang reappeared in Washington in December with her hand held out for another three thousand million dollars and a pledge to stop Communism in Asia. Enough common sense remained to keep the American government from being sucked into this vortex, but not enough to persuade it to turn steadfastly away.

Vainly hoping to capture the initiative, the Truman administration in August 1949 published its White Paper, a cloth-bound volume of four hundred pages of narrative history and six hundred pages of documents. Apologetically, however, the Secretary of State wrote an introduction to the volume endorsing the prejudices of his enemies, the China lobby, pointing an accusing finger at 'Soviet imperialism', and ending with an invocation of the American 'tradition'. In America the enemies of the administration rose easily to the bait; in China Mao Tse-tung dismissed the White Paper as 'a bucket of cold water . . . for those who believe that everything American is good and hope that China will model herself on the United States'.[15] In Peking the People's Republic of China now made its official début; in America, diplomacy, haunted by the ghosts of the past, showed itself ill of the palsy. Paradoxically the United States was deep in the midst of helping the conquered Japanese recover from the stunning blows it had rained upon them, only to be stunned in its turn by the Chinese revolution.

Competence, foresight, understanding of the complex forces at work in China and Japan are the qualities which shine through in the reports and recommendations of the American field service during the critical period between the two World Wars. Misunderstanding, false idealism, lip-service to stereotyped phrases, timidity, bigotry, sheer ignorance and stupidity were, on the other hand, the hallmarks of official policy as determined in Washington. One stands aghast at the enormous discrepancy between the knowledge and intelligence of the one, the childish notions and lofty self-righteousness of the other. 'Because our principles are different' – Henry L. Stimson's stock explanation for passing moral sentence on Japan in 1931 – seems equally applicable to the strictures upon Communist China. In the foreign service reports, as described in the foregoing pages, reside the qualities essential to the true statesman – courage, imagination and the treatment of international politics as the art of the possible.

It is tantalizing, though of course historically otiose, to speculate on what *would have been* the record of American diplomacy in East Asia had it accepted guidance from the embassy and consular staffs in Tokyo, Peking and, later, in Nanking and Chungking. And the question inevitably arises, since the President, the Secretary of State and their Far Eastern advisers were so inattentive to the intelligence supplied by the field service, what was the value of the service? The effect was the same as if the service had been non-existent. Nor can the failure of the government in Washington be explained in terms of the necessity to gratify the prejudices of public opinion – anti-Japanese and anti-communist passions, party politics, pressure from special interest groups like the 'China lobby', and so on. The 'experts' in the government bureaucracy – men whose business it was to be informed – themselves mirrored these prejudices, keeping their minds closed and obstinately refusing even to study the realities. President Roosevelt remained unshaken in his romantic belief in a benevolent alliance with China under Chiang Kai-shek and with Russia under Stalin (America of course dominant among the three). Historical sense is also common sense, but in these men it was a minus quantity. They furnish a perfect example of Hegel's famous dictum: 'Peoples and governments have never learned anything from history.'

In spite of the triumph of the Chinese Communists, moreover, the United States continued to practise the fiction that only Chiang Kai-shek, protected with his Nationalist remnant on his island refuge, was China. Peking, it was solemnly declared, was not Chinese, it was Communist. Chiang alone was the *legitimate* ruler. This was the official stance of the American government twenty years after his flight from the mainland. It calls to mind Louis XIV's support of the Stuart Pretender to the English throne in the years after the Revolution of 1688.

Japan, meanwhile, under the benevolent despotism of General Douglas MacArthur, was conditioned as the starting-point for a Christian crusade against the Communist infidel. As the apostle to the Orient of American 'democracy and Christianity', MacArthur would prepare the Japanese for 'formal conversion to the Christian faith', and utilize their islands as 'a natural base from which in time to advance the Cross through all of Asia'. At his invitation American missionaries flocked to Japan. MacArthur on his part harboured Bonaparte-like ambitions which came to the fore during the Korean War. But attempts to unify Korea under American auspices and make that small country a 'showcase of American democracy' were fated to disappointment. Korea in American hands was from the standpoint of Peking 'a dagger thrust into China's chest', and the United States was now a stand-in for Japan as China's mortal enemy. A swift Chinese intervention in the winter of 1950 put an end to American hopes for a crusade on the mainland and returned Korea to its original post-war division.

In John Foster Dulles, Secretary of State under President Eisenhower, the American crusade against communism found another zealous spokesman. With Metternich-like persistence Dulles pushed forward with his ideas of recruiting the 'legitimate' rulers of East Asia under the banner of the United States. Ignoring the foreign service and treating foreign affairs as his personal domain, the Secretary travelled from one Asian country to another in an effort to construct a grand alliance. At China he brandished the threat of 'massive retaliation' should it molest the American favourite on Taiwan; and in Japan, which was by now demonstrating remarkably recuperative powers, Dulles thought he discerned a useful tool. The progress of that country, however, was enough to indicate that it would not for long remain in the shoes of a subordinate.

Meanwhile a situation in Indo-China similar to that in Korea provided another stage for the warfare against communism. In 1954 Vietnamese Communists triumphed over the French, who then withdrew, leaving an armistice line at the 17th parallel between two *de facto* Vietnamese republics. The United States stepped into the vacuum, throwing its weight behind non-communist South Vietnam, and Secretary Dulles professed a desire for a showdown, using the threat of atomic warfare to coerce the North Vietnamese into surrender. If the Chinese intervened as they had in Korea, Dulles was ready to use the atomic bomb on them too. But President Eisenhower would not embark on this crusade without a pledge of support from Britain and France; and, since the pledge was not forthcoming, the United States for the time accepted the *de facto* situation.

A new wave in this crusade started, however, in 1960 when President Kennedy intervened directly with troops. Eight years later the number of American ground forces on hand in Vietnam had passed the half million mark. As the distinguished authority on Sino-American relations, J. K. Fairbank, put it, this intervention was 'only an updated use of gunboat diplomacy'; but though the struggle was fated to move into still higher levels of ferocity and though it backfired in the form of increasing disaffection and riots in the United States itself, the United States was unable to impose its will upon the North Vietnamese. President Johnson and his Secretary of State were as uncompromising as Dulles and added a new version of the 'yellow peril'. The war in Vietnam, they declared, had to be won, otherwise there would be 'a billion Chinese . . . armed with nuclear weapons'. Thus China was tacitly acknowledged to be the real enemy.

The ludicrous side to this crusade may be seen by taking note of the growing power of Communist China and the attention paid it by the many nations who took exception to the wishes of the United States. Dulles in 1958 insisted that Peking's admission 'would vitiate, if not destroy, the United Nations.' But in 1971 China was voted in and the Chiang Kai-shek régime brusquely expelled. Thus defied, and conscious of the increasing popular resistance to the war at home, the American government under President Nixon began experimenting with new tactics: the President paid personal visits to Peking and to Moscow, but at the same time attempted to isolate and strangle North Vietnam into submission. Thus the United States has signified its intention to remain dominant in South-East Asia, but in the long run its prospects seem dim. China is in a better position than it has been since before the era of Western dominance began, and Japan is again forging to the front. So new questions beg for answers in the tangled affairs of East Asia.

Notes to the text

CHAPTER I
1 J. K. Fairbank, *Trade and Diplomacy on the China Coast. The Opening of the Treaty Ports, 1842-1854* (Cambridge, Massachusetts, 1964), vol. I, p. 29.
2 Mark Mancall, 'The Ch'ing Tribute System: an Interpretative Essay', in J. K. Fairbank, *The Chinese World Order. Traditional China's Foreign Relations* (Cambridge, Massachusetts, 1968), p. 63.
3 Quoted by J. K. Fairbank, *Trade and Diplomacy on the China Coast. The Opening of the Treaty Ports, 1852-1854*, vol. I, p. 59.

CHAPTER II
1 Quoted by James Kirker, *Adventures to China. Americans in the Southern Oceans, 1792-1812* (New York, 1970), p. 4.
2 Delano to Sturgis, 6 April 1843, in the Forbes Collection, Baker Library, Harvard University.
3 See Richard W. Van Alstyne, *Genesis of American Nationalism* (Waltham, Massachusetts, 1970), p. 81.
4 Quoted in Kirker, *op. cit.*, p. 107.
5 See Richard W. Van Alstyne, *The Rising American Empire* (Oxford, 1960), pp. 125-6, for the whole excerpt.
6 Otto von Kotzebue, *A Voyage of Discovery into the South Sea and Bering straits ... in the years 1815-1818* (3 vols, London, 1821), vol. I, p. 280, vol. III, p. 241.
7 *The Missionary Herald*, vol. IX (1813), p. 23.
8 Charles Wilkes, *The Narrative of the United States Exploring Expedition* (5 vols, Philadelphia, 1845), vol. V, pp. 171-2.
9 This and other excerpts from Forbes's letters are taken direct from the Forbes collection, Baker Library, Harvard University.
10 This lecture was delivered in Boston. *Niles Weekly Register* (Baltimore), vol. 61 (1842), pp. 326-30, printed in full.
11 Quoted by Stanley F. Wright, *Hart and the Chinese Customs* (Belfast, 1950), p. 78.

CHAPTER III
1 Quoted by G. B. Sansom, *The Western World and Japan* (New York, 1950), p. 181.
2 Quoted from *The Presbyterian Review* (December 1852) in Edward Yorke McCauley's *Diary, With Perry in Japan*, ed. Allan B. Cole (Princeton, 1942), pp. 19-20.

3 See Richard W. Van Alstyne, *The Rising American Empire* (Oxford, 1960), pp. 173-4, for the whole excerpt.
4 McCauley, *op. cit.*
5 Quoted by Arthur Walworth, *Black Ships off Japan. The Story of Commodore Perry's Expedition* (New York, 1946), p. 39.
6 *Ibid.*, p. 36.
7 See Van Alstyne, *op. cit.*, pp. 174-5.
8 From Marcy's instructions to Harris, printed in Hunter Miller, *Treaties and other International Acts of the United States of America* (8 vols, Washington, D.C., 1931-48), vol. VII, Doc. 191.
9 Harris's Journal appears as Pt II in William Elliot Griffis, *Townsend Harris, First American Envoy to Japan* (Boston and New York, 1895).
10 G. B. Sansom, *The Western World and Japan. A Study in the Interaction of European and Asiatic Cultures* (New York, 1950), p. 301.

CHAPTER IV
1 26 May 1868, *Papers relating to Foreign Affairs*, Pt I.
2 Quoted by Kwang-Ching Liu, *Anglo-American Steamship Rivalry in China, 1862-1874* (Cambridge, Massachusetts, 1962), p. 76.
3 Quoted by Paul A. Cohen, *China and Christianity. The Missionary Movement and the Growth of Chinese Antiforeignism, 1860-1870* (Cambridge, Massachusetts, 1963), p. 46.
4 *Ibid.*, p. 105.
5 Quoted in Richard W. Van Alstyne, *The Rising American Empire* (Oxford, 1960), p. 184.
6 These excerpts are from Paul A. Varg, *Missionaries, Chinese, and Diplomats. The American Protestant Missionary Movement in China, 1890-1952* (Princeton, 1958), pp. 3, 18, 55.
7 Marilyn Blatt Young, *The Rhetoric of Empire. American China Policy, 1895-1901* (Cambridge, Massachusetts, 1968), p. 85.
8 *Ibid.*, p. 87.
9 Excerpts from various California newspapers: *Sacramento Daily Union, Democratic State Journal, Daily Alta California*, et al., examined under my direction by Mr John Copley.

CHAPTER V
1 Stanley Wright, *Hart and the Chinese Customs* (Belfast, 1950), pp. 683, 710-11.

2 Payson J. Treat, *Diplomatic Relations between the United States and Japan* (2 vols, Stanford, 1932), vol. II, pp. 499-500; Marilyn Blatt Young, *The Rhetoric of Empire. American China Policy, 1895-1901* (Cambridge, Massachusetts, 1968), pp. 20-21; Victor Purcell, *The Boxer Uprising* (Cambridge, England, 1963), p. 127.

3 Wright, *op. cit.*, p. 645.

4 Nathan Pelcovits, *Old China Hands and the Foreign Office* (New York, 1969), pp. 258, 302.

5 Charles S. Campbell, *Special Business Interests and the Open Door Policy* (New Haven, Connecticut, 1951), p. 12.

6 Thomas J. McCormick, *China Market. America's Quest for Informal Empire, 1893-1901* (Chicago, 1967), pp. 38, 73.

7 *Ibid.*, p. 107.

8 *Ibid.*, p. 119.

9 Young, *op. cit.*, pp. 101, 104-5.

10 *Ibid.*, pp. 119, 122.

11 Chester C. Tan, *The Boxer Catastrophe* (New York, 1955), pp. 112-13; Purcell, *op. cit.*, p. 252.

12 Paul A. Varg, *Missionaries, Chinese, and Diplomats. The American Protestant Missionary Movement in China, 1890-1952* (Princeton, 1958), p. 116.

13 Whitelaw Reid, *American and English Studies* (New York, 1913), pp. 164-5.

14 Brooks Adams, *America's Economic Supremacy* (New York, 1947), pp. 104-5, 174-5. Quoted by permission of Harper and Row, publishers.

15 J. A. Hobson, *Imperialism. A Study* (London, 1938), p. 368.

16 Charles A. Conant, *The United States in the Orient* (Boston, 1900), p. 222.

17 Edward H. Zabriskie, *American-Russian Rivalry in the Far East* (Philadelphia, 1946), p. 76. Italics for emphasis.

18 Raymond A. Esthus, *Theodore Roosevelt and Japan* (Seattle, 1966), pp. 36-37.

19 Elting E. Morison, ed., *The Letters of Theodore Roosevelt* (8 vols, Cambridge, Massachusetts, 1951-4), vol. IV, pp. 1308-10, 1312-13.

20 Esthus, *op. cit.*, p. 292.

21 Morison, ed., *op. cit.*, vol. V, 698-9.

22 Esthus, *op. cit.*, p. 264.

23 Helen Dodson Kahn, *The Great Game of Empire. Willard D. Straight and American Far Eastern Policy* (Ann Arbor, 1971), p. 59.

24 *Ibid.*, p. 143; Esthus, *op. cit.*, pp. 234-5.

25 Kahn, *op. cit.*, p. 212.

26 *Ibid.*, pp. 313-15, 345.

27 *Ibid.*, p. 546.

CHAPTER VI

1 Quoted by Joseph R. Levenson, *Modern China and its Confucian Past. The Problem of Intellectual Continuity* (Garden City, 1964), p. 82.

2 Helen Dodson Kahn, *The Great Game of Empire. Willard D. Straight and American Far Eastern Policy* (Ann Arbor, 1971), p. 577.

3 Woodrow Wilson, *A History of the American People* (5 vols, New York and London, 1902), vol. V, p. 296.

4 Quoted by Russell H. Fifield, *Woodrow Wilson and the Far East. The Diplomacy of the Shantung Question* (Hamden, 1965), p. 101.

5 Charles Seymour, ed., *Intimate Papers of Colonel House* (4 vols, Boston, 1926-28), vol. III, p. 25.

6 The text of the manifesto is in Chow Tse-tsung, *The May Fourth Movement. Intellectual Revolution in Modern China* (Cambridge, Massachusetts, 1960), p. 106.

CHAPTER VII

1 *Papers relating to the Foreign Relations of the United States*, 1926, vol. I, pp. 671-82. Hereafter referred to as *FRUS*.

2 Paul A. Varg, *Missionaries, Chinese and Diplomats. The American Protestant Missionary Movement in China, 1890-1952* (Princeton, 1958), pp. 180-211.

3 *FRUS*, 1929, vol. II, pp. 145-82.

4 *Ibid.*, 1931, vol. III, pp. 86-7, 315-16.

5 League of Nations. Appeal by the Chinese Government. Report of the Commission of Enquiry (Geneva, 1932), pp. 26-49.

6 *FRUS*, 1931, vol. III, pp. 175, 315-28.

7 *Ibid.*, pp. 45, 47, 343, 409-10, 411, 431-2, 496; 1932, vol. III, p. 27.

8 *Ibid.*, 1932, vol. III, pp. 7-8, 440-42, 457-58; Japan, 1931-1941, vol. I, pp. 83-7.

9 *Ibid.*, 1932, vol. IV, pp. 36-40, 137-40, 143-65, 219-21.

10 *Ibid.*, pp. 229-31, 349.

CHAPTER VIII

1 *FRUS*, 1933, vol. III, p. 195; 1934, vol. III, pp. 160-64, 181-5; Japan, 1931-1941, vol. I, pp. 224-5.

2 *Ibid.*, 1935, vol. III, 306-9; Dorothy Borg, *The United States and the Far Eastern Crisis of 1933-1938* (Cambridge, Massachusetts, 1964), p. 153.

3 *FRUS*, 1934, vol. III, pp. 46-50; Lucien Bianco, *Origins of the Chinese Revolution 1915-1949* (Stanford, 1971), p. 67.

4 Borg, *op. cit.*, pp. 206, 212, 231; Edgar Snow, *Red Star over China* (rev. ed., New York, 1968), pp. 373-96; Lyman P. Van Slyke, *Enemies and Friends. The United Front in Chinese Communist History* (Stanford, 1967), pp. 65-74.

5 Borg, *op. cit.*, pp. 259, 265.

6 Manny T. Koginos, *The Panay Incident: Prelude to War* (Lafayette, 1967), p. 80.

7 *FRUS*, 1937, vol. III, pp. 385-6.
8 *Ibid.*, pp. 588, 591-3, 690-7, 703-4; Borg, *op. cit.*, pp. 366-7, 382, 399-441.
9 *FRUS*, Japan, 1931-1941, vol. II, pp. 9, 34-5, 111-22, 123-8.
10 William L. Langer and S. Everett Gleason, *The Undeclared War 1940-1941* (New York, 1953), pp. 30-32.
11 The documentation for this passage, and for the remainder of this chapter, is to be found in *FRUS*, Japan, 1931-1941, and especially in *FRUS*, 1941, vols IV-V.

CHAPTER IX
1 The documentation for these pages on the Chungking régime is in *FRUS*, 1942, China, especially pp. 13-16, 24-5, 27-8, 109-14, 212-26.
2 Ping-ti Ho, *Studies in the Population of China, 1368-1953* (Cambridge, Massachusetts, 1959), p. 271.
3 Lucien Bianco, *Origins of the Chinese Revolution 1915-1949*, trans. Muriel Bell (Stanford, 1971), pp. 50, 75. I considered the last sentence significant enough to be italicised.
4 *FRUS*, 1942, China, pp. 19-22; Cordell Hull, *Memoirs* (2 vols, New York, 1948), vol. II, p. 1587; Tang Tsou, *America's Failure in China 1941-1950* (Chicago, 1963), pp. 37-8.

5 Quoted by Tsou, *op. cit.*, p. 52.
6 *FRUS*, 1942, China, pp. 524-6; *United States Relations with China* (Department of State Publication 3573, Washington, D.C., 1949), pp. 488-91. Hereafter referred to as *The White Paper*.
7 *FRUS*, 1943, China, pp. 191-399, prints these many reports in full.
8 Barbara W. Tuchman, *Stilwell and the American Experience in China, 1911-1945* (New York, 1970), p. 300.
9 The quotations are from Charles F. Romanus and Riley Sunderland, *Stilwell's Command Problems* (Department of the Army, Washington, D.C., 1956), pp. 302, 431-3, 463; and from Tuchman, *op. cit.*, pp. 345-7, 386, 501.
10 Robert E. Sherwood, *Roosevelt and Hopkins. An Intimate History* (New York, 1948), p. 870; *The White Paper*, pp. 113-14.
11 Tuchman, *op. cit.*, p. 522; *The White Paper*, pp. 311 ff.
12 *The White Paper*, pp. 313, 581-4; Tuchman, *op. cit.*, pp. 523-6; Tsou, *op. cit.*, pp. 289-94, 343-5.
13 *The White Paper*, pp. 132, 315-23, 338, 814; also Bianco, *op. cit.*, pp. 159, 167-98, and Tsou, *op. cit.*, pp. 349-493.
14 Tsou, *op. cit.*, pp. 469, 490-92.
15 Mao Tse-tung, *Selected Works* (4 vols, Peking, 1968), vol. IV, p. 430.

Selective bibliography

CHAPTER I
For general histories of China on which I have relied extensively see: J. K. Fairbank, ed., *The Chinese World Order. Traditional China's Foreign Relations* (Cambridge, Massachusetts, 1968); Wolfgang Franke, *China and the West. The Cultural Encounter, 13th to 20th Centuries*, trans. R. A. Wilson (New York, 1967); René Grousset, *The Rise and Splendour of the Chinese Empire* (Berkeley and Los Angeles, 1968); Dun J. Li, *The Ageless Chinese, A History* (New York, 1965); K. M. Panikkar, *Asia and Western Dominance. A Survey of the Vasco da Gama Epoch of Asian History, 1498-1945* (London, 1953); Edwin O. Reischauer and J. K. Fairbank, *East Asia. The Great Tradition* (Boston, 1958).
On Marco Polo see: *The Travels of Marco Polo* (New York, 1958); Henry H. Hart, *Marco Polo* (Norman, 1967).
On Confucius see: *The Analects of Confucius*, trans. and annotated Arthur Waley (New York, 1938); *Confucianism in Action*, ed. David S. Nevison and Arthur F. Wright (Stanford, 1959).

CHAPTER II

On fitting the American advance into East Asia into the larger picture of American empire building in the eighteenth to the twentieth centuries see: Richard W. Van Alstyne, *The Rising American Empire* (Oxford, 1960); William A. Williams, ed., *From Colony to Empire: Essays in the History of American Foreign Relations* (New York, 1972).

On Hawaii and Pacific exploration and trade see: Harold Whitman Bradley, *The American Frontier in Hawaii. The Pioneers, 1789-1843* (Stanford, 1942); William Davis Robinson, *Memoirs of the Mexican Revolution... Some Observations on the Practicality of opening a Commerce between the Pacific and Atlantic Oceans... and of the Vast Importance of such Commerce to the Civilized World* (2 vols, London, 1821); David B. Taylor, *The Wilkes Expedition. The First United States Exploring Expedition (1838-1842)* (Philadelphia, 1968).

On Americans and the opium trade see: Jacques M. Downs, 'American Merchants and the China Opium Trade, 1800-1840', *Harvard Business Review*, vol. 42 (1968), pp. 418-42; Arthur Waley, *The Opium War through Chinese Eyes* (New York, 1958); Peter W. Fay, 'The Protestant Mission and the Opium War', *Pacific Historical Review*, XL (May 1971), pp. 145-62.

CHAPTER III

Samuel Eliot Morison, '*Old Bruin*', *Commodore Matthew Calbraith Perry, 1794-1858* (Boston, 1967); William Elliot Griffis, *Townsend Harris, First American Envoy to Japan* (Boston and New York, 1895); Henry Heuskin, *Japan Journal, 1855-1861*, trans. and ed. Jeannette C. van der Corput and Robert A. Wilson (New Brunswick, New Jersey, 1964).

CHAPTER IV

John Walton Caughey, *California* (New York, 1953), pp. 449-55; Rodman W. Paul, 'The Origin of the Chinese Issue in California', *Miss. Valley Hist. Rev.*, XXV (1938), 181-96; Elmer C. Sandemeyer, *The Anti-Chinese Movement in California* (Urbana, 1939).

CHAPTER V

Howard K. Beale, *Theodore Roosevelt and the Rise of America to World Power* (Baltimore, 1956); William Reynolds Braisted, *The United States Navy in the Pacific, 1897-1909* (Austin, 1958); John W. Foster, *Diplomatic Memoirs* (2 vols, Boston, 1909); Fred Harvey Harrington, *God, Mammon and the Japanese. Dr Horace N. Allen and Korean-American Relations, 1884-1905* (Madison, 1944); Seward W. Livermore, 'American Naval Base Policy in the Far East, 1850-1914', *Pac. Hist. Rev.*, XIII, 1944, pp. 113-35; William L. Langer, *The Diplomacy of Imperialism* (New York, 1960); Cyril Pearl, *Morrison of Peking* (Sydney, 1967); C. F. Remer, *A Study of Chinese Boycotts, with Special Reference to their Economic Effectiveness* (Baltimore, 1933); Richard W. Van Alstyne, 'Myth versus Reality in the Far Eastern Policies of the United States', *International Affairs*, vol. 32 (July 1956), pp. 287-97; Charles Vevier, *The United States and China, 1906-1913. A Study of Finance and Diplomacy* (New Brunswick, New Jersey, 1955).

CHAPTERS VI, VII and VIII

Dorothy Borg, *American Policy and the Chinese Revolution, 1925-1928* (New York, 1947); William R. Braisted, *The United States Navy in the Pacific 1909-1922* (Austin, 1971); Herbert Feis, *The China Tangle* (Princeton, 1953) and *The Road to Pearl Harbor. The Coming of the War between the United States and Japan* (Princeton, 1950); Joseph C. Grew, *Turbulent Era. A Diplomatic Record of Forty Years, 1904-1945* (2 vols, Boston, 1952); Cordell Hull, *Memoirs* (2 vols, New York, 1948); Yamato Ichihashi, *Japanese in the United States. A Critical Study of the Problems of the Japanese Immigrants and their Children* (Stanford, 1932); F. C. Jones, *Japan's New Order in East Asia, its Rise and Fall, 1937-1945* (Oxford, 1945); Charles B. McLane, *Soviet Policy and the Chinese Communists, 1931-1946* (New York, 1958); Paul

W. Schroeder, *The Axis Alliance and Japanese-American Relations* (Ithaca, 1958); Richard W. Van Alstyne, *American Crisis Diplomacy. The Quest for Collective Security, 1918-1952* (Stanford, 1952); John Chalmers Vinson, *The Parchment Peace. The United States and the Washington Conference, 1921-1922* (Athens, Georgia, 1955).

CHAPTER IX AND EPILOGUE
Warren I. Cohen, *America's Response to China. An Interpretative History of Sino-American Relations* (New York, 1971); Chalmers A. Johnson, *Peasant Nationalism and Communist Power. The Emergence of Revolutionary China, 1937-1945* (Stanford, 1962); John W. Spanier, *The Truman-MacArthur Controversy and the Korean War* (Cambridge, Massachusetts, 1959); General Albert C. Wedemeyer, *Wedemeyer Reports!* (New York, 1958); H. Bradford Westerfield, *Foreign Policy and Party Politics. Pearl Harbor to Korea* (New Haven, Connecticut, 1955); Allen S. Whiting, *China Crosses the Yalu. The Decision to Enter the Korean War* (Stanford, 1960); *The Pentagon Papers, or the Secret History of the Vietnam War* (New York, 1971).

List of illustrations

Index